Mobil ★★
Travel Guide

WHERE TO
EAT
CHICAGO

FROM MOBIL FIVE-STARS TO STREET BITES

Ethnic Eateries   Food Festivals   Star Chefs   Bars   Maps

Acknowledgements

We gratefully acknowledge the help of our representatives for their efficient and perceptive inspections of the dining establishments listed; the establishments' proprietors for their cooperation in showing their facilities and providing information about them; and the many users of Mobil Travel Guide's products who have taken the time to share their experiences. We are also grateful to all the highly talented writers who contributed entries to this book.

Vice President, Publications: Kevin Bristow

Director, Editorial Content: Pam Mourouzis

Director of Publishing Production Services: Ellen Tobler

Editors: Brenda McLean, Nancy Swope

Publishing Coordinator: Shawn McNichols

Restaurant Research and Compilation: Meira Chiesa

Concept Design: Chris Mulligan

Cover Design: Kellie Bottrell/ The Brochure Factory

Maps: © MapQuest.com, Inc. This product contains proprietary property of MapQuest.com, Inc. Unauthorized use, including copying, of this product is expressly prohibited.

Printing Acknowledgment: North American Corporation of Illinois

www.mobiltravelguide.com

Although every effort has been made to verify the information contained herein, restaurants can close or change without warning. Before making your plans, please call the restaurant to verify that it is still open and to confirm the cuisine type, meals served, and other particulars of importance to you. Some restaurants that appear on the maps in this book may not appear in the final listing. The publisher assumes no responsibility for inconsistencies or inaccuracies in the data and assumes no liability for any damages of any type arising from errors or omissions.

ISBN: 0-7627-3597-X

Manufactured in the United States of America.

10 9 8 7 6 5 4 3 2 1

Contents

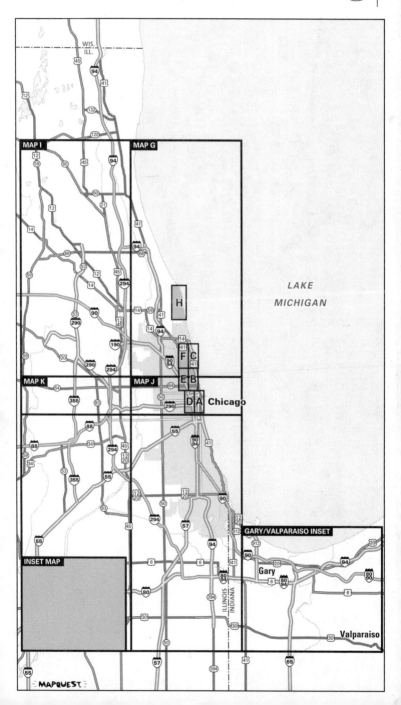

HILL ST

MAPLE ST

CEDAR ST
BELLEVUE PL

Oak
Street
Beach

Walter Payton College
Preparatory HS

OAK ST
WALTON ST

Washington
Square Park

LOCUST ST

CHESTNUT ST

INSTITUTE PL

CHICAGO

Moody
Bible
Institute

SUPERIOR ST

DELAWARE ST

TOOKER PL CHESTNUT ST

PEARSON ST

WALTON ST

ERNST CT

DEARBORN

AV

ST

ST

DELAWARE

Seneca
Park

SUPERIOR

LAKE SHORE DR

Lake Shore
Park

Northwestern
University

Northwestern
Memorial Hosp

VA Lakeside
Medical Center

MIES VAN DER

ROHE WAY

Outer
Harbor

Ohio
Street
Beach

CHICAGO

HURON ST

ERIE

ONTARIO ST

McCLURG

CT

ST

Olive
Park

FRANKLIN ST

LA SALLE ST

OHIO ST

CAMPBELL PL

ILLINOIS ST

HUBBARD ST

KINZIE ST

STATE ST

WABASH

RUSH ST

CITY PLAZA

ST. CLAIR ST

GRAND AV

OHIO ST

ILLINOIS ST

GRAND AV

COLUMBUS DR

PARK DR

NEW

NORTH
WATER ST

Chicago
Maritime
Museum

ILLINOIS
ST

Navy
Pier

ORLEANS ST

WACKER DR

Chicago River

WACKER DR

STETSON AV

HARBOR DR-N

41

N

POST PL

WELLS ST

LA SALLE ST

CLARK ST

GARVEY CT

COUCH PL

HADDOCK PL

LAKE

BENTON PL

BEAUBIEN CT

S. WATER ST

FIELD BL

COUCH PL

COURT PL

WASHINGTON ST

CALHOUN ST

MADISON ST

ARCADE PL

MONROE ST

Daley
Center

DEARBORN ST

HOLDEN CT

GARLAND CT

Prudential
Building

RANDOLPH

Chicago
Cultural
Center

American Conservatory
Of Music

The Art
Institute
of Chicago

Daley
Plaza

MONROE DR

LAKE
MICHIGAN

Petrillo
Bandshell

MARBLE PL

ADAMS ST

QUINCY ST

JACKSON

Sears
Tower

Post
Office

Federal
Office
Building

The Symphony
Center

Roosevelt
University-
Chicago

FRANKLIN DR

CHICAGO TRANSIT AUTHORITY

CONGRESS PLAZA DR

BL

Grant
Park

Chicago
Harbor

Buckingham
Fountain

FINANCIAL PL

CONGRESS

PKWY

HARRISON ST

Jones Metropolitan
HS Business & Commerce

Columbia
College

Spertus
Institute of
Jewish Studies

BALBO DR

WELLS ST

FINANCIAL PL

LA SALLE ST

DEARBORN ST

PLYMOUTH CT

Dearborn
Park

POLK ST

8TH ST

9TH ST

STATE ST

COLUMBUS DR

LAKE SHORE DR

TAYLOR ST

11TH ST

ROOSEVELT

CLARK ST

FEDERAL ST

PLYMOUTH

13TH ST

WABASH RD

13TH ST

14TH ST

INDIANA AV

41

WM L MC FETRIDGE DR

Shedd
Aquarium

MUSEUM
CAMPUS

Field
Museum

SOLIDARITY DR

Northerly
Island Park

0   .125   .25 mi
0   .125   .25 km

MAPQUEST

1 312 Chicago
136 N Lasalle St
Chicago, IL 60602

2 Aria
200 N Columbus Dr
Chicago, IL 60601

3 Atwood Café
1 W Washington Blvd
Chicago, IL 60602

22 Avenues
108 E Superior
Chicago, IL 60611

23 Bandera
535 N Michigan Ave
Chicago, IL 60611

4 The Berghoff
17 W Adams St
Chicago, IL 60603

26 Bice
158 E Ontario St
Chicago, IL 60611

27 Bin 36
339 N Dearborn St
Chicago, IL 60610

28 Brasserie Jo
59 W Hubbard St
Chicago, IL 60610

31 Butterfield 8
711 N Wells St
Chicago, IL 60610

34 Cafe Iberico
739 N Lasalle Dr
Chicago, IL 60610

35 Caliterra
633 N St. Clair St
Chicago, IL 60611

37 Cantare
200 E Chestnut
Chicago, IL 60611

38 Cape Cod Room
140 E Walton Pl
Chicago, IL 60611

39 The Capital Grille
633 N St. Clair St
Chicago, IL 60611

40 Carmine's
1043 N Rush St
Chicago, IL 60611

41 Cerise
520 N Michigan Ave
Chicago, IL 60611

43 Chicago Chop House
60 W Ontario St
Chicago, IL 60610

46 Coco Pazzo
300 W Hubbard St
Chicago, IL 60610

48 Crofton On Wells
535 N Wells St
Chicago, IL 60610

49 Cyrano's Bistrot and Wine Bar
546 N Wells St
Chicago, IL 60610

50 The Dining Room
160 E Pearson St
Chicago, IL 60611

52 Ed Debevic's
640 N Wells St
Chicago, IL 60610

53 Eli's The Place for Steak
215 E Chicago Ave
Chicago, IL 60611

54 Erawan
729 N Clark St
Chicago, IL 60611

5 Everest
440 S Lasalle St
Chicago, IL 60605

57 Fogo de Chão
661 N Lasalle St
Chicago, IL 60610

58 Frontera Grill
445 N Clark St
Chicago, IL 60610

60 Gene & Georgetti
500 N Franklin St
Chicago, IL 60610

61 Gibson's Steakhouse
1028 N Rush St
Chicago, IL 60611

6 Gioco
1312 S Wabash Ave
Chicago, IL 60605

62 Harry Caray's
33 W Kinzie St
Chicago, IL 60610

63 Hatsuhana
160 E Ontario St
Chicago, IL 60611

65 Heaven on Seven on Rush
600 N Rush St
Chicago, IL 60611

70 Joe's Be-Bop Cafe
600 E Grand Ave
Chicago, IL 60611

72 Keefer's
20 W Kinzie
Chicago, IL 60610

73 Kevin
9 W Hubbard
Chicago, IL 60610

74 Kiki's Bistro
900 N Franklin St
Chicago, IL 60610

7 La Strada
155 N Michigan Ave
Chicago, IL 60601

79 Lawry's The Prime Rib
100 E OntarioSt
Chicago, IL 60611

80 Le Colonial
937 N Rush St
Chicago, IL 60611

81 Les Nomades
222 E Ontario St
Chicago, IL 60611

82 Maggiano's Little Italy
516 N Clark St
Chicago, IL 60610

86 Mike Ditka's
100 E Chestnut St
Chicago, IL 60611

87 mk
868 N Franklin St
Chicago, IL 60610

90 Morton's Of Chicago
1050 N State St
Chicago, IL 60610

91 Nacional 27
325 W Huron
Chicago, IL 60610

92 Naha
500 N Clark St
Chicago, IL 60610

93 Naniwa
607 N Wells
Chicago, IL 60610

8 Nick's Fishmarket
51 S Clark St
Chicago, IL 60603

94 Nix
163 E Walton Pl
Chicago, IL 60611

95 Nomi
800 N Michigan Ave
Chicago, IL 60611

97 Oak Tree
900 N Michigan Ave
Chicago, IL 60611

9 Opera
1301 S Wabash Ave
Chicago, IL 60605

10 Palm
323 E Wacker Dr
Chicago, IL 60601

245 Pane Caldo
72 E Walton St
Chicago, IL 60611

99 Papagus Greek Taverna
620 N State St
Chicago, IL 60610

11 Petterino's
150 N Dearborn St
Chicago, IL 60601

101 Pili Pili
230 W Kinzie St
Chicago, IL 60610

102 Pizzeria Uno
29 E Ohio St
Chicago, IL 60611

106 Redfish
400 N State St
Chicago, IL 60610

107 Riva
700 E Grand Ave
Chicago, IL 60611

108 Roy's
720 N State
Chicago, IL 60610

12 Russian Tea Time
77 E Adams St
Chicago, IL 60603

110 Saloon
200 E Chestnut St
Chicago, IL 60611

113 Sayat Nova
157 E Ohio St
Chicago, IL 60611

115 Seasons
120 E Delaware Pl
Chicago, IL 60611

116 Shanghai Terrace
108 E Superior
Chicago, IL 60610

117 Shaw's Crab House
21 E Hubbard St
Chicago, IL 60611

119 Signature Room at the 95th
875 N Michigan Ave
Chicago, IL 60611

120 Spiaggia
980 N Michigan Ave
Chicago, IL 60611

122 Su Casa
49 E Ontario St
Chicago, IL 60611

123 Sushi Samba Rio
504 N Wells St
Chicago, IL 60610

124 SWK
710 N Wells St
Chicago, IL 60610

125 Szechwan East
340 E Ohio St
Chicago, IL 60611

126 Tizi Melloul
531 N Wells St
Chicago, IL 60610

128 Topolobampo
445 N Clark St
Chicago, IL 60610

13 Trattoria No. 10
10 N Dearborn St
Chicago, IL 60602

129 TRU
676 N Saint Clair St
Chicago, IL 60611

130 Tucci Benucch
900 N Michigan Ave
Chicago, IL 60611

14 Vivere
71 W Monroe St
Chicago, IL 60603

132 Vong's Thai Kitchen
6 W Hubbard
Chicago, IL 60610

133 Wave
644 N Lake Shore Dr
Chicago, IL 60611

16 Abu Nawas
2411 N Clark St
Chicago, IL 60614

17 Adobo Grill
1610 N Wells St
Chicago, IL 60614

18 Ambria
2300 Lincoln Park W
Chicago, IL 60614

30 Bricks
1909 N Lincoln Ave
Chicago, IL 60614

32 Cafe Ba-Ba-Reeba!
2024 N Halsted St
Chicago, IL 60614

33 Cafe Bernard
2100 N Halsted St
Chicago, IL 60614

42 Charlie Trotter's
816 W Armitage Ave
Chicago, IL 60614

51 Dinotto Ristorante
215 W North Ave
Chicago, IL 60610

55 erwin
2925 N Halsted St
Chicago, IL 60657

59 Geja's Cafe
340 W Armitage Ave
Chicago, IL 60614

64 Heat
1507 N Sedgwick
Chicago, IL 60610

77 La Creperie
2845 N Clark St
Chicago, IL 60657

88 Mon Ami Gabi
2300 N Lincoln Park W
Chicago, IL 60614

89 Monsoon
2813 N Broadway
Chicago, IL 60657

96 North Pond
2610 N Cannon Dr
Chicago, IL 60614

98 Orange
3231 N Clark St
Chicago, IL 60657

104 Pump Room
1301 N State Pkwy
Chicago, IL 60610

111 Salpicon
1252 N Wells St
Chicago, IL 60610

112 Sauce
1750 N Clark St
Chicago, IL 60614

121 Stanley's
1970 N Lincoln Ave
Chicago, IL 60614

127 Topo Gigio Ristorante
1516 N Wells St
Chicago, IL 60610

**131 Twin Anchors Restaurant
and Tavern**
1655 N Sedgwick St
Chicago, IL 60614

MAP C

LAKE MICHIGAN

LAKE SHORE DR

MAGNOLIA AV
BROADWAY
WINTHROP AV
KENMORE AV
SHERIDAN RD
BERWYN AV

14 FOSTER AV

41 ST

Goudy Sch
WINONA ST

CARMEN AV
WINNEMAC AV
MAGNOLIA AV

Marti Bilingual Education Center

CARMEN AV
ARGYLE ST

41

MARGATE TER

AINSLIE ST
AINSLIE ST

McCutcheon Sch

CASTLEWOOD TER

Chicago Lakeshore Hospital

GUNNISON ST
LAWRENCE

GUNNISON ST
AV

LAWRENCE DR

LAWRENCE-WILSON DR

SIMONDS DR

RACINE AV
CLIFTON AV
MAGNOLIA AV

LAKESIDE PL
LELAND AV
EASTWOOD AV

MARINE DR

WILSON DR

WILSON AV

Truman College

WINDSOR AV
SUNNYSIDE AV

SUNNYSIDE AV

CLIFTON AV

AGATITE AV

CLARENDON AV
DAYTON ST
HAZEL ST

Clarendon Community Park

MONTROSE DR

MONTROSE HARBOR DR

Montrose Harbor

BROADWAY

PENSACOLA AV
CULLOM AV

JUNIOR TER

Brenneman Sch

Graceland Cemetery

KENMORE AV

JUNIOR TER
HUTCHINSON ST

Uptown Library

BUENA AV

First German Lutheran Cemetery

SEMINARY AV
KENMORE
SHERIDAN RD

GORDON TER
BELLE PLAINE AV

GORDON TER

Disney Magnet Sch

Lincoln Park

CUYLER AV

BITTERSWEET PL

IRVING PARK RD

Thorek Hospital & Medical Center

19

MARINE DR

RECREATION DR

Wunder's Cemetery

DAKIN ST

CHICAGO

Hebrew Cemetery

BYRON ST

SHERIDAN RD

Gill Park

RACINE AV
CLIFTON AV
SEMINARY AV
KENMORE AV
SHEFFIELD AV

GRACE ST

BRADLEY PL

WILTON AV
FREMONT ST

BROADWAY
PINE GROVE AV

BELMONT HARBOR DR

LAKE SHORE DR

Bird Sanctuary

WAVELAND AV

Le Moyne Sch

PATTERSON AV

PATTERSON AV

Wrigley Field

ADDISON ST

CLARK ST

Chicago Transit Authority

RETA AV
HALSTED ST

BROMPTON AV
CORNELIA AV

EDDY ST
CORNELIA AV

STRATFORD PL

NEWPORT AV

ELAINE PL

HAWTHORNE PL

41

CLIFTON AV
SEMINARY AV
KENMORE AV

100

85

20
44

ROSCOE ST

BUCKINGHAM PL

DAYTON ST

ALDINE AV

ALDINE AV

135

MELROSE ST

Belmont Harbor

0 .125 .25 mi
0 .125 .25 km

N

MAPQUEST

MAP C

xiii

20   **Arco de Cuchilleros**
3445 N Halsted St
Chicago, IL 60657

44   **Chicago Diner**
3411 N Halsted St
Chicago, IL 60657

85   **Mia Francesca**
3311 N Clark St
Chicago, IL 60657

100   **Penny's Noodle Shop**
3400 N Sheffield Ave
Chicago, IL 60657

135   **Yoshi's Café**
3257 N Halsted St
Chicago, IL 60657

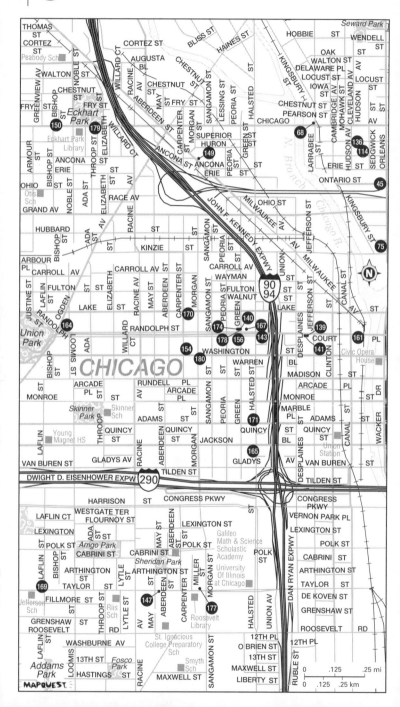

139 avec
615 W Randolph St
Chicago, IL 60661

140 Azuré
832 W Randolph St
Chicago, IL 60607

141 Blackbird
619 W Randolph St
Chicago, IL 60606

143 Bluepoint Oyster Bar
741 W RandolphSt
Chicago, IL 60661

147 Chez Joel
1119 W Taylor St
Chicago, IL 60607

45 Chilpancingo
358 W Ontario St
Chicago, IL 60610

149 Como
695 N Milwaukee Ave
Chicago, IL 60622

150 Flo
1434 W Chicago Ave
Chicago, IL 60622

68 Japonais
600 W Chicago Ave
Chicago, IL 60610

75 Klay Oven
414 N Orleans St
Chicago, IL 60610

154 La Sardine
111 N Carpenter St
Chicago, IL 60607

156 Marche
833 W Randolph St
Chicago, IL 60607

161 Nine
440 W Randolph St
Chicago, IL 60606

164 one sixtyblue
160 N Loomis
Chicago, IL 60607

165 Parthenon
314 S Halsted St
Chicago, IL 60661

167 Redlight
820 W Randolph St
Chicago, IL 60607

169 Rosebud
1500 W Taylor St
Chicago, IL 60607

170 Rushmore
1023 W Lake St
Chicago, IL 60607

171 Santorini
800 W Adams St
Chicago, IL 60607

114 Scoozi
410 W Huron
Chicago, IL 60610

174 Sushi Wabi
842 W Randolph St
Chicago, IL 60607

177 Tuscany
1014 W Taylor St
Chicago, IL 60612

178 Vivo
838 W Randolph St
Chicago, IL 60607

179 West Town Tavern
1329 W Chicago Ave
Chicago, IL 60622

180 Wishbone
1001 W Washington Blvd
Chicago, IL 60607

136 Zealous
419 W Superior St
Chicago, IL 60610

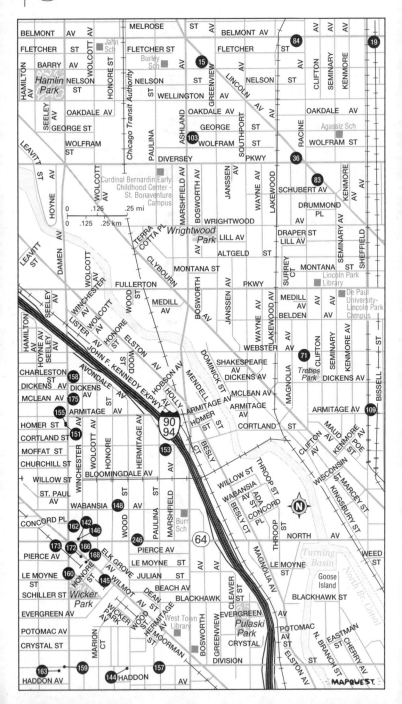

15 A La Turka
3134 N Lincoln Ave
Chicago, IL 60657

19 Ann Sather
929 W Belmont Ave
Chicago, IL 60657

142 Blue Fin
1952 W North Ave
Chicago, IL 60622

144 Bob San
1805-07 W Division
Chicago, IL 60622

145 Bongo Room
1470 N Milwaukee Ave
Chicago, IL 60622

146 Cafe Absinthe
1954 W North Ave
Chicago, IL 60622

36 Calliope Cafe
2826 N Lincoln Ave
Chicago, IL 60657

148 Club Lucky
1824 W Wabansia Ave
Chicago, IL 60622

151 Glory
1952 N Damen Ave
Chicago, IL 60647

153 Jane's
1655 W Cortland St
Chicago, IL 60622

71 John's Place
1202 W Webster Ave
Chicago, IL 60614

155 Le Bouchon
1958 N Damen Ave
Chicago, IL 60647

157 Mas
1670 W Division St
Chicago, IL 60622

83 Maza
2748 N Lincoln Ave
Chicago, IL 60657

84 Menagerie
1232 W Belmont
Chicago, IL 60657

158 Meritage
2118 N Damen Ave
Chicago, IL 60647

159 Mirai Sushi
2020 W Division St
Chicago, IL 60622

160 MOD.
1520 N Damen Ave
Chicago, IL 60622

162 Northside Cafe
1635 N Damen Ave
Chicago, IL 60647

163 Ohba
2049 W Division St
Chicago, IL 60622

166 Piece
1927 W North Ave
Chicago, IL 60622

246 Pot Pan
1750 W North Ave
Chicago, IL 60622

103 Prego Ristorante
2901 N Ashland Ave
Chicago, IL 60657

168 Rodan
1530 N Milwaukee Ave
Chicago, IL 60622

109 Sai Café
2010 N Sheffield Ave
Chicago, IL 60614

172 Souk
1552 N Milwaukee Ave
Chicago, IL 60622

173 Spring
2039 W North Ave
Chicago, IL 60647

175 Toast
2046 N Damen Ave
Chicago, IL 60647

Rosehill Cemetery

RASCHER AV
BOWMANVILLE AV
SUMMERDALE AV
FARRAGUT AV
FOSTER AV

RASCHER
BALMORAL AV
SUMMERDALE AV
BERWYN AV
FARRAGUT AV
Trumbull Sch
FOSTER AV

CAMPBELL AV
ARTESIAN AV
WESTERN AV
BELL AV
HOYNE AV
DAMEN AV
HONORE ST
GLENWOOD AV
WAYNE AV
LAKEWOOD AV

78
56

41

WINONA ST
CARMEN AV
CARMEN AV
WINNEMAC AV
ARGYLE ST
AINSLIE ST
GUNNISON ST

Chappell Sch
Amundsen HS
Winnemac Park

WINONA ST
WINONA ST
CARMEN AV
WINNEMAC AV

ARGYLE ST
AINSLIE ST
AINSLIE ST

LINCOLN AV
OAKLEY AV
CLAREMONT AV
BELL AV
LEAVITT ST
HAMILTON AV
HOYNE AV
SEELEY AV
WINCHESTER AV
WOLCOTT AV
Chicago Transit Authority
RAVENSWOOD

Methodist Hospital of Chicago

JANSSEN AV
Bezalian Library

69
21

0   .125   .25 mi
0   .125   .25 km

LAWRENCE AV

CAMPBELL AV
ARTESIAN AV
GIDDINGS ST
McPherson Sch
LELAND AV
EASTWOOD AV
WILSON AV
WINDSOR AV
SUNNYSIDE AV
AGATITE AV
MONTROSE AV

CLAREMONT AV
OAKLEY AV
HAMILTON AV
SEELEY AV

Waters Sch
Stitzey Regional Library
Welles Park

Chase Park

HERMITAGE AV
PAULINA ST
ASHLAND AV
CLARK ST
DOVER ST
BEACON ST
MALDEN ST
GREENVIEW AV

Stockton Sch

CHICAGO

76 **25**
118

PENSACOLA AV
CULLOM AV
HUTCHINSON ST
BERTEAU AV
WARNER AV
BELLE PLAINE AV
CUYLER AV
IRVING PARK RD

CAMPBELL AV
CLAREMONT AV
Cooley Sch
WOLCOTT AV

PENSACOLA AV
CULLOM AV
HUTCHINSON ST
WARNER AV
BELLE PLAINE AV
CUYLER AV
IRVING PARK RD

Ravenswood Sch
Mary Ethel Courtenay Spec. Educ. Facility
Lake View HS

HONORE ST
RAVENSWOOD

N

Revere Park
DAKIN ST
BYRON ST
BERENICE AV

BRADLEY PL
WAVELAND AV

ADDISON ST
EDDY ST
NEWPORT AV
HENDERSON ST
SCHOOL ST
MELROSE ST

OAKLEY AV
BELL AV
LEAVITT ST
HAMILTON AV
HOYNE AV
SEELEY AV
DAMEN AV
ARTESIAN AV
WESTERN AV
CLAREMONT AV
CAMPBELL AV

Bell Sch
Devry Institute of Tech-Chicago

LARCHMONT AV
BERENICE AV
GRACE ST
BRADLEY PL
PATTERSON AV

19

BYRON ST
GRACE ST
Blaine Sch

134

29

RAVENSWOOD
HERMITAGE AV
MARSHFIELD AV
ASHLAND AV
BOSWORTH AV
GREENVIEW AV
JANSSEN AV
SOUTHPORT AV
WAYNE AV
LAKEWOOD AV

St Andrew Sch
Hamilton Sch

CORNELIA AV
ROSCOE ST
HENDERSON ST
SCHOOL ST
MELROSE ST

Sheil Park

47

P.O.

US 41

MAPQUEST

21 Atlantique
5101 N Clark St
Chicago, IL 60640

25 Bella Domani
4603 N Lincoln Ave
Chicago, IL 60625

29 Brett's
2011 W Roscoe St
Chicago, IL 60618

47 Coobah
3423 N Southport Ave
Chicago, IL 60657

56 Finestra di Calo
5341 N Clark St
Chicago, IL 60640

69 Jin Ju
5203 N Clark St
Chicago, IL 60640

76 La Bocca Della Verita
4618 N LincolnAve
Chicago, IL 60618

78 La Tache
1475 W Balmoral Ave
Chicago, IL 60640

118 She She
4539 N Lincoln Ave
Chicago, IL 60625

134 Xippo
3759 N Damen
Chicago, IL 60618

221 94th Aero Squadron
9335 Skokie Blvd
Skokie, IL 60077

137 Amarind's
6822 W North Ave
Chicago, IL 60607

138 Arun's
4156 N Kedzie Ave
Chicago, IL 60618

201 Bank Lane Bistro
670 Bank Ln
Lake Forest, IL 60045

24 Basta Pasta
6733 Olmstead St
Chicago, IL 60631

204 Betise
1515 N Sheridan Rd
Wilmette, IL 60091

195 Cafe Central
455 Central Ave
Highland Park, IL 60035

217 Cafe La Cave
1038 Waukegan Rd
Northbrook, IL 60062

229 Café Le Coq
734 Lake St
Oak Park, IL 60301

196 Carlos'
429 Temple Ave
Highland Park, IL 60035

214 Ceiling Zero
2124 Northbrook Ct
Northbrook, IL 60062

205 Convito Italiano
1515 N Sheridan Rd
Wilmette, IL 60091

212 Country Inn Restaurant at
Lambs Farm
1519 Wagner Rd
Glenview, IL 60025

198 Del Rio
228 Green Bay Rd
Highwood, IL 60040

202 English Room
255 E Illinois St
Lake Forest, IL 60045

199 Froggy's
306 Green Bay Rd
Highwood, IL 60040

200 Gabriel's
310 Green Bay Rd
Highwood, IL 60040

66 Hema's Kitchen
6406 N Oakley Ave
Chicago, IL 60645

67 Indian Garden
2546 W Devon Ave
Chicago, IL 60659

152 Ixcapuzalco
2919 N Milwaukee Ave
Chicago, IL 60618

247 Michael's Restaurant
1879 Second St
Highland Park, IL 60035

210 mk North
305 Happ Rd
Northfield, IL 60093

105 Ras Dashen
5846 N Broadway
Chicago, IL 60660

203 South Gate Cafe
655 Forest Ave
Lake Forest, IL 60045

216 Tonelli's
254 Skokie Blvd
Northbrook, IL 60062

176 Tre Kronor
3258 W Foster Ave
Chicago, IL 60625

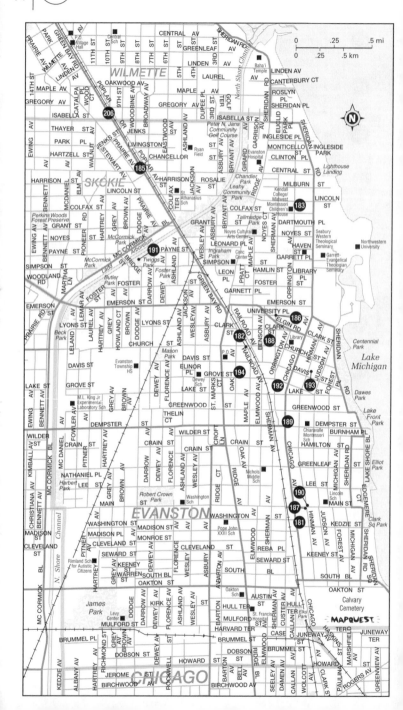

181 Campagnola
815 Chicago Ave
Evanston, IL 60202

182 Carmen's
1012 Church St
Evanston, IL 60201

183 The Dining Room at
Kendall College
2408 Orrington Ave
Evanston, IL 60201

185 Jilly's Cafe
2614 Green Bay Rd
Evanston, IL 60201

186 Las Palmas
817 University Pl
Evanston, IL 60201

187 Lucky Platter
514 Main St
Evanston, IL 60202

188 Merle's #1 Barbecue
1727 Benson St
Evanston, IL 60201

189 New Japan
1322 Chicago Ave
Evanston, IL 60201

190 Oceanique
505 Main St
Evanston, IL 60202

191 Pete Miller's Steakhouse
1557 Sherman Ave
Evanston, IL 60201

192 Prairie Moon
1502 Sherman Ave
Evanston, IL 60201

193 Trio
1625 Hinman Ave
Evanston, IL 60201

194 Va Pensiero
1566 Oak Ave
Evanston, IL 60201

206 Walker Brothers Original
Pancake House
153 Green Bay Rd
Wilmette, IL 60091

MAP I

xxiv

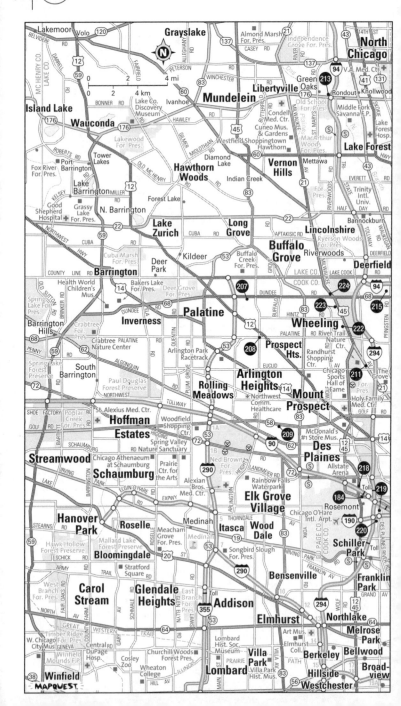

MAP I

xxv

206 Bob Chinn's Crab House
1070 S Milwaukee Ave
Wheeling, IL 60090

218 Carlucci
2777 Mannheim Rd
Des Plaines, IL 60018

223 Don Roth's
393 S Milwaukee Ave
Wheeling, IL 60090

184 Don's Fishmarket
10275 W Higgins Rd
Rosemont, IL 60018

215 Francesco's Hole in the Wall
500 Anthony Trail
Northbrook, IL 60062

207 Le Titi de Paris
1015 W Dundee Rd
Arlington Heights, IL 60004

219 Meson Sabika
61 N Milwaukee Ave
Wheeling, IL 60090

220 Morton's of Chicago
6111 N River Rd
Rosemont, IL 60018

220 Nick's Fishmarket
9525 W Bryn Mawr Ave
Rosemont, IL 60018

208 Palm Court
1912 N Arlington Heights Rd
Arlington Heights, IL 60004

211 Periyali Greek Taverna
9860 Milwaukee Ave
Glenview, IL 60016

209 Retro Bistro
1746 W Golf Rd
Mt. Prospect, IL 60056

213 Tavern in the Town
At Jct I-94 and Hwy 176
Libertyville, IL 60048

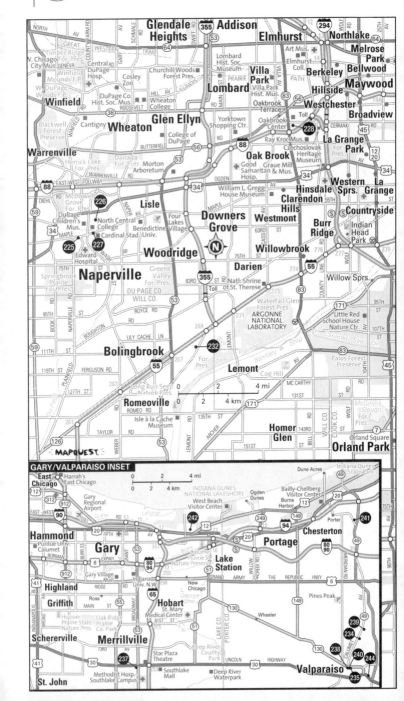

234 Billy Jack's Café and Grill
2904 N Calumet Ave
Valparaiso, IN 46383

235 Bistro 157
157 Lincolnway
Valparaiso, IN 46383

227 Braxton Seafood Grill
22 E Chicago Ave
Naperville, IL 60540

237 Café Venezia
405 W 81st Ave
Merrillville, IN 46410

238 Clayton's
66 W Lincolnway
Valparaiso, IN 46383

239 Dish Restaurant
3907 Calumet Ave
Valparaiso, IN 46383

240 Don Quixote
119 E Lincolnway
Valparaiso, IN 46383

228 Fond de la Tour
3 Oak Brook Center Mall
Oak Brook, IL 60523

241 Lucrezia
428 S Calumet Rd
Chesterton, IN 46304

242 Miller Bakery Café
555 S Lake St
Gary, IN 46403

225 Raffi's on 5th
1025 Aurora Ave
Naperville, IL 60540

226 Samba Room
200 E 5th Ave
Naperville, IL 60563

244 Strongbow Inn
2405 E Hwy 30
Valparaiso, IN 46383

232 White Fence Farm
11700 Joliet Rd
Lemont, IL 60439

CHICAGO MAP LEGEND

METRO MAPS

CONTROLLED ACCESS HIGHWAYS

Free

Toll; Toll Booth

Under Construction

Interchange & Exit Number

Rest Area; Service Area
Grey with facilities

OTHER HIGHWAYS

Primary Highway

Secondary Highway

Multilane Divided Highway
Primary and secondary highways only

Other Paved Road

HIGHWAY MARKERS

Interstate Route

U.S. Route

State Route

County or Other Route

Business Route

OTHER SYMBOLS

Airport

Forest and/or Park

Trail

Point of Interest

Visitor Information

Public/Private Golf
Professional tournament location

Hospital

Ski Area

National & State Capital

County Seat

Cities & Populated Places
Type size indicates relative importance

Urban Area

CITY MAPS

HIGHWAYS

Freeway & Tollway

Primary Highway

Other Paved Road

HIGHWAY MARKERS

Interstate Route

U.S. Route

State Route

County or Other Route

Business Route

Parks

Point of Interest

Railroads

ALL MAPS

Restaurant Locations

Introduction

Whether you're traveling to a city you've never visited or simply exploring a new area of town, one of the greatest joys of travel is eating. From gooey slices of pizza enjoyed standing up at the counter to plates of amazingly fresh sushi savored in an elegant and upscale restaurant, food brings instant gratification. Even if lousy weather threatens to ruin your trip, a great meal can save the day and brighten your mood instantly.

Food has been near and dear to our hearts at Mobil Travel Guide for the last 46 years. That's why we're so pleased to announce our newest series of books, focused exclusively on dining. We've highlighted the very best places to eat in Chicago, from fine-dining establishments to casual, family-friendly restaurants to hip and trendy hotspots. Pasta, steak, curry, dim sum—you name it, we've got it covered.

This book isn't just a boring A-to-Z list of restaurants, either. We tell you about the city's well-known chefs and specialties so that if your time is limited, you can sample the foods that really shine here. We include information about food-related attractions, from cooking schools to factory tours to shops that sell the latest kitchen gadgets. And we list some of the city's best groceries, markets, and bakeries so that you can take a little piece of Chicago home with you.

Our goal was to make this book as easy to use as possible. After an introduction to the city's dining scene, you'll find restaurant listings broken down by area of the city. Following the listings for the city itself are listings for outlying areas, again arranged geographically. Within each section, restaurants are listed alphabetically. If you're searching for a restaurant that is budget-friendly, that is suitable for a business meal, that invites romance, or that meets other special criteria, you'll find a variety of specialized indexes, as well as a general index, at the back of the book to help you find just the right spot.

The Mobil One- to Five-Star Ratings for Restaurants

The proprietary Mobil One- to Five-Star rating system, the oldest and most respected restaurant, hotel, and spa inspection and rating program in North America, puts us head and shoulders above other dining guides. We don't rely on the opinions of restaurant critics, whom restaurants often shower with special attention that a "normal" diner would never receive. And our star ratings are not based on popularity.

Definitions

The Mobil Star ratings for restaurants are defined as follows:

✪ ★ ★ ★ ★ ★ : A Mobil Five-Star restaurant offers one of few flawless dining experiences in the country. These establishments consistently provide their guests with exceptional food, superlative service, elegant décor, and exquisite presentations of each detail surrounding a meal.

✪ ★ ★ ★ ★ : A Mobil Four-Star restaurant provides professional service, distinctive presentations, and wonderful food.

✪ ★ ★ ★ : A Mobil Three-Star restaurant offers good food, warm and skillful service, and enjoyable décor.

✪ ★ ★ : A Mobil Two-Star restaurant serves fresh food in a clean setting with efficient service. Value is considered in this category, as is family friendliness.

✪ ★ : A Mobil One-Star restaurant provides a distinctive experience through culinary specialty, local flair, or individual atmosphere.

Allow us to emphasize that we do not charge establishments for inclusion in our guides. We have no relationship with any of the restaurants or businesses we list and rate; we act only as a consumer advocate. In essence, we do the investigative legwork so that you won't have to. We experience the restaurant as an average consumer would, receiving no special treatment and no discounts.

Approach

Since its founding in 1958, Mobil Travel Guide has served as an advocate for travelers seeking knowledge about hotels, restaurants, and places to visit. Based on an objective process, we make recommendations to our customers that we believe will enhance the quality and value of their travel experiences. Our process of rating each establishment includes:

- ✪ Unannounced facility inspections
- ✪ Incognito service evaluations for Mobil Four-Star and Mobil Five-Star properties
- ✪ Review of consumer feedback
- ✪ Senior management oversight

For each property, more than 450 attributes, including cleanliness, physical facilities, and employee attitude and courtesy, are measured and evaluated to produce a mathematically derived score, which is then blended with the other elements to form an overall score. These quantifiable scores allow comparative analysis among properties and form the basis that we use to assign our Mobil One- to Five-Star ratings.

This process focuses largely on guest expectations, guest experience, and consistency of service, not just physical facilities. It rewards those properties that continually strive for and achieve excellence each year.

Only facilities that meet Mobil Travel Guide's standards earn the privilege of being listed. Deteriorating facilities, run-of-the-mill restaurants or poorly managed establishments are not rated. A Mobil Travel Guide rating constitutes a quality recommendation from our staff; every listing is an accolade, a recognition of achievement. We strive to identify excellence within each star category, incorporating a commitment to diversity and variety throughout the Mobil One- to Five-Star Ratings.

All listed establishments have been inspected by experienced field representatives and/or reviewed by a senior incognito evaluator. Rating categories reflect both the features a property offers and its quality in relation to similar establishments across the country.

About the Restaurant Listings

All Mobil Star-rated restaurants listed in this book have a full kitchen and offer tables where you may sit to dine with a complete menu. In addition to a Mobil Star rating, each listing includes the restaurant's address, phone and fax numbers, and Web site (if it has one). We tell you the cuisine type, days of operation (if not open daily year-round), meals served, and price category. We also indicate if the restaurant does not accept credit cards and if valet parking is available. The price categories are defined as follows, per person, and assume that you order an appetizer or dessert, an entrée, and one drink:

○ **$$$$** = $86 and up
○ **$$$** = $36-$85
○ **$$** = $16-$35
○ **$** = $15 and under

At the ends of some listings, we include an icon that provides further information:

○ 🔲 : The restaurant is not easily accessible to persons in wheelchairs or with otherwise limited mobility.

Although we recommend every restaurant we list in this book, a few stand out—they offer noteworthy local specialties or stand above the others in their category in quality, value, or experience. To draw your attention to these special spots, we've included the spotlight icon to the left of the listing, as you see here.

Keep in mind that the hospitality business is ever-changing. Restaurants—particularly small chains and standalone establishments—change management or even go out of business with surprising quickness. Although we make every effort to double-check information frequently, we nevertheless recommend that you call ahead to make sure the place you've selected is open and offers what you're looking for.

Tipping Guide

Tips are expressions of appreciation for good service. However, you are never obligated to tip if you receive poor service.

Before tipping in a restaurant, carefully review your check for any gratuity or service charge that is already included in your bill. If you're in doubt, ask your server.

Here are some general guidelines for tipping in restaurants:

- Coffee shop and counter service waitstaff usually receive 15 percent of the bill, before sales tax.
- In full-service restaurants, tip 18 percent or more of the bill, where deserving, before sales tax.
- In fine restaurants, where gratuities are shared among a larger staff, 18 to 20 percent is appropriate.
- In most cases, the maitre d' is tipped only if the service has been extraordinary, and only on the way out. At upscale restaurants in major metropolitan areas, $20 is the minimum.
- If there is a wine steward (sommelier), tip $20 for exemplary service, or more if the wine was decanted or the bottle was very expensive.
- Tip $1 to $2 per coat at the coat check.
- Tip valet parking staff $1 to $2.

Send Us Your Feedback

We hope that your travels are enjoyable and relaxing and that this book helps you get the most out of every meal you eat. If any aspect of your experience with this book motivates you to comment, please drop us a line. We depend a great deal on our readers' remarks, so you can be assured that we will read your comments and factor them into our research. General comments about our books are also welcomed. You can send an e-mail to info@mobiltravelguide.com or write to us at:

Mobil Travel Guide
1460 Renaissance Dr, Suite 401
Park Ridge, IL 60068

Mobil Four- and Five-Star Restaurants in This Book

★ ★ ★ ★ ★ Restaurants

Charlie Trotter's

Trio, *Evanston*

★ ★ ★ ★ Restaurants

Ambria

Crofton on Wells

The Dining Room

Everest

Les Nomades

Seasons

Spring

Tru

Chicago

Rudyard Kipling wrote of Chicago, "I have struck a city—a real city—and they call it Chicago." For poet Carl Sandburg, it was the "City of the Big Shoulders"; for writer A. J. Liebling, a New Yorker, it was the "Second City." Songwriters have dubbed it a "toddlin' town" and "my kind of town." Boosters say it's "the city that works"; and to most people, it is "the Windy City." But over and above all the words and slogans is the city itself and the people who helped make it what it is today.

The people of Chicago represent a varied ethnic and racial mix: Native Americans gave the city its name—Checagou; restless Easterners traveled here in search of land and opportunity; hundreds of thousands of venturesome immigrants from Europe, Asia, and Latin America came here and brought the foods and customs of the Old World; and Southern blacks and Appalachians came with hopes of finding better jobs and housing. All of these unique groups have contributed to the strength, vitality, and cosmopolitan ambience that make Chicago a distinctive and special experience for visitors.

Chicago's past is equally distinctive, built on adversity and contradiction. The first permanent settler was a black man, Jean Baptiste Point du Sable. The city's worst tragedy, the Great Fire of 1871, was the basis for its physical and cultural renaissance. In the heart of one of the poorest ethnic neighborhoods, two young women of means, Jane Addams and Ellen Gates Starr, created Hull-House, a social service institution that has been copied throughout the world. A city of neat frame cottages and bulky stone mansions, it produced the geniuses of the Chicago School of Architecture (Louis Sullivan, Daniel Burnham, Dankmar Adler, William LeBaron Jenney, and John Willborn Root), whose innovative tradition was carried on by Frank Lloyd Wright and Ludwig Mies van der Rohe. Even its most famous crooks provide a study in contrasts: Al Capone, the Prohibition gangster, and Samuel Insull, the financial finagler whose stock manipulations left thousands of small investors penniless in the late 1920s.

Chicago's early merchants resisted the intrusion of the railroad, yet the city became the rail center of the nation. Although Chicago no longer boasts a stockyard, its widely diversified economy makes it one of the most stable cities in the country. Metropolitan Chicago has more than 12,000 factories with a $20 billion annual payroll and ranks first in the United States in the production of canned and frozen foods, metal products, machinery, railroad equipment, letter-press printing, office equipment, musical instruments, telephones, housewares, candy, and lampshades. It has one of the world's busiest airports, the largest grain exchange, and the biggest mail-order business. It is a great educational center (58 institutions of higher learning); one of the world's largest convention and trade show cities; a showplace, marketplace, shopping, and financial center; and a city of skyscrapers, museums, parks, and churches, with more than 2,700 places of worship.

Chicago turns its best face toward Lake Michigan, where a green fringe of parks forms an arc from Evanston to the Indiana border. The Loop is a city within a city, with many corporate headquarters, banks, stores, and other enterprises. To the far south are the docks along the Calumet River, used by ocean vessels since the opening of the St. Lawrence Seaway and servicing a belt of factories, steel mills, and warehouses. Behind these lies a maze of industrial and shopping areas, schools, and houses.

Although Louis Jolliet mapped the area as early as 1673 and du Sable and a compatriot, Antoine Ouilmette, had established a trading post by 1796, the real growth of the city did not begin until the 19th century and the onset of the Industrial Revolution.

In 1803, the fledging US government took possession of the area and sent a small military contingent from Detroit to select the site for a fort. Fort Dearborn was built at a strategic spot on the mouth of the Chicago River; on the opposite bank, a settlement slowly grew. Fort and settlement were abandoned when the British threatened them during the War of 1812. On their way to Fort Wayne, soldiers and settlers were attacked and killed or held captive by Native Americans who had been armed by the British. The fort was rebuilt in 1816; a few survivors returned and new settlers arrived, but there was little activity until Chicago was selected as the terminal site of the proposed Illinois and Michigan Canal. This started a land boom.

Twenty thousand Easterners swept through on their way to the riches of the West. Merchants opened stores; land speculation was rampant. Although 1837—the year Chicago was incorporated as a city—was marked by financial panic, the pace of expansion and building did not falter. In 1841, grain destined for world ports began to pour into the city; almost immediately, Chicago became the largest grain market in the world. In the wake of the grain came herds of hogs and cattle for the Chicago slaughterhouses. Tanneries, packing plants, mills, and factories soon sprang up.

The Illinois and Michigan Canal, completed in 1848, quadrupled imports and exports. Railroads fanned out from the city, transporting merchandise throughout the nation and bringing new produce to Chicago. During the slump that followed the panic of 1857, Chicago built a huge wooden shed (the Wigwam) at the southeast corner of Wacker and Lake to house the Republican National Convention. Abraham Lincoln was nominated Republican candidate for president here in 1860. The Civil War doubled grain shipments from Chicago. In 1865, the mile-square Union Stock Yards were established. Chicago was riotously prosperous; its population skyrocketed. Then, on October 8, 1871, fire erupted in a cow barn and roared through the city, destroying 15,768 buildings, killing almost 300 people, and leaving a third of the population homeless. But temporary and permanent rebuilding started at once, and Chicago emerged from the ashes to take advantage of the rise of industrialization. The labor unrest of the period produced the Haymarket bombing and the Pullman and other strikes. The 1890s were noteworthy for cultural achievements: orchestras, libraries, universities, and the new urban architectural form for which the term "skyscraper" was coined. The Columbian Exposition of 1893, a magnificent success, was followed by depression and municipal corruption.

Chicago's fantastic rate of growth continued into the 20th century. Industries boomed during World War I, and in the 1920s the city prospered as never before—unruffled by dizzying financial speculation and notorious gang warfare, an outgrowth of Prohibition. The stock market crash of 1929 brought down the shakier financial pyramids; the repeal of Prohibition virtually ended the rackets; and a more sober Chicago produced the Century of Progress Exposition in 1933. Chicago's granaries and steel mills helped carry the country through World War II. The past several decades have seen a reduction of manufacturing jobs in the area and an increase of jobs in service industries and in the fields of finance, law, advertising, and insurance. The 1996 relocation of Lake Shore Drive made it possible to create the Museum Campus, a 57-acre extension of Burnham Park. The Museum Campus provides an easier and more scenic route to the Adler Planetarium, Field Museum, and Shedd Aquarium, surrounding them with one continuous park featuring terraced gardens and broad walkways.

Although, in the eyes of some, Chicago evokes the image of an industrial giant, it is also a city in which the arts flourish. Chicagoans are proud of their world-famous symphony orchestra, their Lyric Opera, and their numerous and diverse dance companies. Since 1912, Chicago has been the home of *Poetry* magazine. Chicago's theater community is vibrant, with more than 100 off-Loop theaters presenting quality drama. The collections at the Art Institute, Museum of Contemporary Art, Terra Museum of American Art, and many galleries along Michigan Avenue and in the River North area are among the best in the country.

Other museums are equally renowned: the Museum of Science and Industry, the Field Museum of Natural History, the Chicago Children's Museum at Navy Pier, and the various specialty museums that reflect the ethnic and civic interests of the city.

The zoos, planetarium, and aquarium, as well as many parks and beaches along the lakefront, afford pleasure for visitors of all ages. Chicago's attractions are many, and sightseeing tours can be taken by boat, bus, car, bicycle, or foot.

Buses and rapid transit lines are integrated into one system—the most extensive in the nation—with interchangeable transfers. Elevated lines run through the Loop. Subway trains run under State and Dearborn streets and run on elevated structures to both the north and the south. Rapid transit lines also serve the west side as well as O'Hare and Midway airports. Commuter trains stretch out to the far western and southern suburbs and near the Wisconsin and Indiana borders.

Driving and parking in Chicago are no more (or less) difficult than in any other major city. There are indoor and outdoor parking areas near and in the Loop; some provide shuttle bus service to the Loop or to the Merchandise Mart.

The Chicago Dining Scene

Chicago has an energy that beats to the drum of a meal. Sure, there are other things to do in this husky, sprawling city of big shoulders. Spend a day at one of the city's excellent museums—but be sure to pause for lunch. Try a roasted vegetable salad at the Butterfly Café in the Peggy Notebaert Nature Museum while looking out at the surrounding trees and the Lincoln Park lagoon. Or savor a steaming bowl of chili in the Adler Planetarium's window-filled Galileo's restaurant while you watch waves crash against Lake Michigan's breakwater.

Take in world-class shopping along Michigan Avenue—and while you're in Water Tower Place, grab a bao (a steamed, filled Chinese bun) at Wow Bao. Or go to Foodlife, Chicago's largest food court, and pick up spicy tacos, Southern-style cornbread, heart-healthy offerings, Thai, Italian, or any number of other unusual dishes.

Feel like award-winning theater? In this city, it's a must. So are the restaurants with pre- and post-dinner theater menus, the restaurants with dessert menus, and the cafés with wine-and-cheese menus.

Whatever your time frame, craving, or budget, you'll find it in Chicago. Although it's no longer just a city of steak and pizza, steak and pizza are still top choices for locals and visitors alike. During the 1950s and 1960s, Chicago was home to dozens of steakhouses, each characterized by—yes—red-flocked wallpaper and dark paneling. In the 1970s and 1980s, they went the way of the fern bar, but today they're back (sans fuzzy wallpaper), and the good ones are exceptionally popular. Arnie Morton has franchised his concept in select cities, but the original is here and the crowds love it.

As for pizza, deep-dish is the name of the game. You're in the town where it all began. Pizza wasn't well known before World War II, but when servicemen fighting in Italy brought the idea back home, it began to gain in popularity. A Chicagoan named Ike Sewell decided to expand on the idea by taking meat, vegetables, cheeses, and spices, and placing them atop a thick, buttery crust to create a meal instead of a snack. In 1943, Sewell opened his first restaurant, Pizzeria Uno, and Chicagoans took to it like wildfire. This eat-it-with-a-knife-and-fork concept proved so popular that he opened a second restaurant, Pizzeria Due, a block away. The restaurants still have lines out the doors, and have been joined by a number of other popular deep-dish Chicago favorites.

In the winter, it's easy to find a cozy pub with a fireplace or two. In the summer, every café in the city with two square feet of sidewalk gets a license and creates outdoor seating. And who can overlook Chicago's plethora of festivals, held every weekend from spring through fall? Neighborhood ethnic fests abound, and the corresponding eats are mouthwatering and plentiful.

And of course, many of the major festivals held in Chicago's Grant Park are centered around food. For ten days in late June and early July, dozens of restaurants bring samples of their best and brightest menu offerings to an explosion of flavor called the Taste of Chicago. Only at

this food fest can you pick up a grilled lobster tail with roasted potatoes at one booth and a Polish sausage at another. The Taste is the
world's greatest sampling menu. And after consuming duck with lingonberries and sauerkraut or toasted cheese ravioli, savvy Taste-goers
know to save room for a chocolate-dipped frozen banana or, better
yet, a hunk of Eli's cheesecake, brought in directly from the original
Eli's The Place for Steak restaurant just off the city's Magnificent Mile.

Got the idea? No? Then how about wandering into one of the city's
ethnic offerings, found anywhere from sleek downtown dining rooms
to don't-blink-or-you'll-miss-it neighborhood storefronts. Satisfy
a craving for deli or diner. Try Chinese, Korean, or sushi. Go French,
Mexican, Spanish, Mongolian, Irish, Greek, or German. Vietnamese,
anyone? Swedish? Chilean? Afghani? Or—now, here's a concept—how
about a big, juicy burger and fries?

restaurants to watch

The following restaurants are still too new to earn a Mobil Star
rating, but these hot new openings are sure to generate buzz.

Andalucia
1820 W Montrose Ave
773/334-6900
A BYOB spot aiming for the most authentic tapas in town.

Darwin's
1935 N Damen Ave
773/772-3719
Popular with the local crowd, Darwin's is a fun getaway for
good food and drinks.

Moto
945 W Fulton Market Ave
312/491-0058
www.motorestaurant.com
Upscale avant-garde cuisine from a pair of Charlie Trotter's alums.

Park Grill
11 N Michigan Ave
312/521-PARK
This contemporary American restaurant has been almost as
anticipated as the park in which it resides.

Pluton
873 N Orleans St
312/266-1440
The much-anticipated northside bistro from chef Jacky Pluton.

Saiko
1307 S Wabash Ave
312/922-2222
A large Japanese steak and sushi joint for the South Loop crowd.

Square Kitchen
4600 N Lincoln Ave
773/751-1500
A chic yet comfortable bistro by longtime Chicago restaurateurs.

Tre Via
1575 N Milwaukee Ave
773/227-7990
This new Wicker Park restaurant features stylish Italian-inspired cuisine and an even better lounge.

Vermilion
10 W Hubbard St
312/527-4060
This River North spot is Chicago's first Latin-Indian fusion restaurant.

Viand Bar and Kitchen
155 E Ontario St
312/255-8505
www.viandchicago.com
With a martini list featuring "culinary cocktails," this place is soon to become a must-see.

Loop and Vicinity

At the center of Chicago, bordered by the Chicago River to the north and west and Roosevelt Road to the south, is the Loop, home to first-rate museums, restaurants, and theaters; financial institutions that move the world's markets; a towering skyline emboldened by an eclectic mix of architecture; and miles of parks and beaches stretching alongside the cool blue waters of Lake Michigan. Named for the loop of elevated trains (commonly referred to as the "El") that run around the downtown area, the Loop represents Chicago's diversity and duality: contemporary and traditional, cosmopolitan and blue-collar, urban and lush. The Loop possesses all of these qualities and more.

Visitors to the Loop could lose themselves for hours—if not days—in the city's internationally acclaimed museums, most of which are within walking distance of one another. Where Adams Street meets Michigan Avenue, you'll find stone steps flanked by a pair of lion sculptures that lead up to the Art Institute of Chicago. This world-renowned museum houses more than 300,000 works of art, including 33 paintings by Claude Monet. Walk south through Grant Park to Buckingham Fountain, a Chicago landmark and one of the largest fountains in the world, with 133 jet sprays and a water capacity of 1.5 million gallons. The Field Museum of Natural History can be found at the south end of Grant Park. Here you can visit Sue, the world's biggest and best preserved Tyrannosaurus rex fossil. Back outside, look southward and appreciate a clear view of historic Soldier Field, home to the NFL's legendary Chicago Bears. A short stroll east leads to Shedd Aquarium, with its dolphins, beluga whales, and other water-loving wildlife. Head a few hundred feet east along the lakefront to Adler Planetarium, a wonderful place to learn about constellations and space exploration.

Some of the world's greatest actors take to the stage in Chicago's theater district in the north Loop. You can choose from shows at a variety of venues, including the Shubert Theatre, Oriental Theater, and Goodman Theatre. Opera aficionados need only venture a few blocks west to the Civic Opera House on North Wacker Drive. Classical music buffs should head over to Orchestra Hall at the corner of Adams Street and Michigan Avenue.

"State Street, that great street." So sang Frank Sinatra, and shopping lovers will no doubt agree with Old Blue Eyes. Marshall Field's flagship store on State Street is the second-largest department store in the world. The store's Great Clock, cast in bronze and affixed to the exterior in 1897, was immortalized by Norman Rockwell when he included it in a painting for the cover of the *Saturday Evening Post*. A couple blocks south, an ornate iron façade outside Carson Pirie Scott greets visitors to another State Street must-stop shopping locale.

The Sears Tower stands tall amid Chicago's Financial District. With a skydeck at 1,353 feet, a clear day presents visitors with the chance to see four states—Illinois, Indiana, Michigan, and Wisconsin. With the Mercantile Exchange, Board of Trade, and Midwest Stock Exchange all nearby, you're bound to see traders in colorful jackets bustling around this district in addition to the many shoppers.

Government buildings can be found in the heart of the Loop. Visit the Daley Center on West Washington Street to view another Chicago landmark, Picasso's unnamed and unpainted 50-foot sculpture. Head a block to the northwest and enter the Thompson Center, glassy and futuristic in design, with a 16-story atrium that's certain to lift your spirits, even on the bleakest January day.

The Loop is not known for its residential neighborhoods, but that may change if recent trends continue. In the South Loop, Printer's Row, with its quiet, tree-lined streets, has established itself as a popular place to live, particularly for those seeking a short commute to work in the city. Many of the print shops in the area have been converted into upscale lofts and trendy restaurants. Likewise, lofts abound on the revitalized west side of the Loop, where Oprah Winfrey produces her popular daytime talk show at Harpo Studios on Washington Boulevard.

Those looking to visit one of Chicago's famed ethnic neighborhoods need not venture far from the Loop. Chinatown sits at the south end, while you can find Little Italy to the southwest. Both offer innumerable restaurant choices, enabling diners to indulge in ethnic cuisines within a stone's throw of the Chicago skyline.

chefs, celebrity, and chicago

"The Hog Butcher to the World," as Chicago was once known, has always been home to an abundance of restaurants. From the meat-and-potatoes charm of its Midwestern locale to the influences of the many immigrant communities, Chicagoans have never had a problem finding a bite to eat.

In the last ten to fifteen years, however, the city's restaurant scene has experienced a renaissance that has caused the rest of the country to sit up and take notice. Whether you're in the Gold Coast, the North Side, or Bucktown, you're sure to find a chef who is garnering rave reviews.

Charlie Trotter paved the way for the current generation of restaurant talent when he opened his eponymous restaurant in a tony Lincoln Park brownstone more than 15 years ago. In his kitchen, he has traded in traditional heavy sauces made with cream and butter for lighter vegetable juice reductions and vinaigrettes. Standard three-plate meals are replaced with a series of miniature courses that challenge the palate. His multi-course tasting menus—with up to 15 individual courses—have predated the current small-plate trend of dining by more than a decade. But food is only one component of the flawless fine dining experience Charlie Trotter has created—the level of service here is second to none. This is the type of restaurant where it's not uncommon to find the servers giving tours of the kitchen and wine cellar, ordering theater tickets, or hailing cabs for guests. It's no wonder Charlie Trotter's is one of the world's great restaurants.

The kitchen team of **Rick Tramonto and Gale Gand** first came to prominence with the opening of Trio in Evanston. It was here that Chicago—and the rest of the nation—first got a look at the whimsical creativity of this duo. And they haven't stopped innovating yet. After establishing Trio as a restaurant to watch, they went on to open and close the charming Brasserie T before taking the plunge back into fine dining with the opening of Tru in June of 1999. Here, they are continuing in the style they pioneered early on. Multi-course collections of creative dishes are presented on unusual china pieces like the famous caviar staircase and individual Versace demitasse soup cups. A carpaccio of octopus might be served on a slab of cold, polished granite, while an almost traditional shrimp cocktail will be served on top of a fish bowl with a live gold-fish swimming underneath. It is this creativity and originality that will keep these two in the public eye for years to come.

Although one of the largest Mexican communities outside of Mexico City is found in Chicago, the cuisine has rarely been thought of as anything more than burritos and tacos—that is, until **Rick Bayless** came along. After completing studies of Spanish and Latin American cultures and spending six years in Mexico, Bayless came to Chicago in 1987 and introduced the city to contemporary Mexican cooking with the opening of Frontera Grill. Two years later, its more formal counterpart, Topolobampo, was opened next door. Both restaurants have raised Mexican cuisine to a level of fine dining not seen in Chicago—or the country—before and have established Rick Bayless as one of the world's foremost authorities on regional Mexican cuisine. His wildly successful restaurants have won many accolades, as have his cookbooks and his television show, *Mexico: One Plate at a Time.*

Perhaps no other chef, however, has personified the surge in creative cookery in Chicago better than **Grant Achatz** of Trio, located in Evanston. After attending the prestigious Culinary Institute of America in New York, Achatz got his professional start at Charlie Trotter's. It was at the world-renowned French Laundry in the Napa Valley, though, where he worked his way up to Sous Chef for the legendary Thomas Keller and solidified his extraordinary technique. Since taking on his first executive chef position at Trio, this unusually young chef has electrified the national restaurant scene with his groundbreaking experi-mentations in avant-garde cuisine. In constantly exploring new territories in cooking—turning out dishes with ingredi-ents like rosemary vapors, tomato powder, and horseradish gellée—Achatz is leading Chicago and the rest of the country into new frontiers of flavor.

And the list goes on: **Roland Liccioni** of Les Nomades. **Suzy Crofton** of Crofton on Wells. **Michael Kornick** of MK. **Sarah Stegner** of the Dining Room at the Ritz-Carlton. Every year, another new chef bursts onto the reinvigorated Chicago restau-rant scene and gives local diners another reason not to cook at home. It's no wonder many consider the Windy City to be one of the great restaurant cities of the world.

Restaurants in the Loop and Vicinity

★ ★ 312 CHICAGO   ❶ (MAP A)
136 N LaSalle St (60602)
Phone 312/696-2420
Fax 312/236-0153
Named for Chicago's urban area code, 312 Chicago is adjacent to the Hotel Allegro in the heart of the Loop's business, shopping, and theater district. The tempting menu marries fresh, contemporary Italian fare with more rustic options. The bilevel setting is clubby yet airy, with a bustling open kitchen and an aromatic rotisserie. The restaurant also serves upscale breakfast and lunch, and the chic bar is a great spot for cocktails. American menu. Menu changes seasonally. Closed Jan 1, Thanksgiving, Dec 25. Breakfast, lunch, dinner. Bar. Casual attire. **$$**

★ ★ ★ ARIA   ❷ (MAP A)
200 N Columbus Dr (60601)
Phone 312/444-9494
www.ariachicago.com
Globetrotting food in a trendy setting make Aria one of the city's more fashionable eateries. Although it's lodged in the Fairmont Chicago, Aria distances itself from the bland stereotype of hotel restaurants by maintaining a street entrance to encourage local patrons to visit. Aria's Asian-inspired décor features Tibetan artwork, orchids, and plush upholstery, underscoring the menu's Eastern orientation. Chef James Wierzelewski formerly worked in Thailand and Malaysia, influences that show up in steamed black bass and crispy duck leg confit, although Indian, Italian, and French notes also flavor the fare. The bar serves a small-bites menu to the cocktail crowd. Eclectic/International menu. Breakfast, lunch, dinner. **$$$**
🅳

★ ★ ATWOOD CAFÉ   ❸ (MAP A)
1 W Washington Blvd (60602)
Phone 312/368-1900
Fax 312/357-2875
www.atwoodcafe.com
The whimsical ground-floor occupant of the Burnham Hotel, Atwood draws a cross-section of travelers, desk jockeys, theatergoers, and shoppers in for chef Heather Terhune's café menu. Modern dishes like grilled calamari and tuna carpaccio balance such comfort food classics as grilled pork chops with spaetzle. Soak up the Loop scene

through floor-to-ceiling windows framing the downtown bustle at lunch, and romantic, marquee-lit streetscapes at dinner. Cozy velvet banquettes and settees encourage lingering. American menu. Closed holidays. Breakfast, lunch, dinner, brunch. Bar. Children's menu. Casual attire. Outdoor seating. **$$**

★ THE BERGHOFF (MAP A)

17 W Adams St (60603)
Phone 312/427-3170
Fax 312/427-6549
www.berghoff.com

The Loop's beloved Berghoff, a landmark of 100-plus years, mingles tourists and locals alike. Out-of-towners line up for the German restaurant's lavishly trimmed dining room where warm potato salad accompanies oversized weiner schnitzel and smoky sausages. Office workers pack the long, wood-paneled barroom slugging mugs of the house beer and munching carved roast beef sandwiches. The bar proudly displays the city's first post-Prohibition liquor license. German menu. Lunch, dinner. Closed Sun; holidays. Bar. Children's menu. Casual attire. **$$**

chinatown

Though not as large as New York's or San Francisco's, Chicago's Chinatown is a vibrant and lively cultural center that makes for a fascinating visit. Located south of the Loop at Cermak and Wentworth, Chinatown's boundary is marked by a tiled gateway and traditional architecture that is reflected in the smallest details, such as the rooftops, lampposts, and phone booths. Within a 10-block radius are 10,000 community members, more than 40 restaurants, 20 gifts shops, herbal and tea stores, and bakeries. Locals tend to visit on Sunday mornings for dim sum, but it's also fun to be in the neighborhood during any of the traditional festivals, including Chinese New Year, the Dragon Boat Festival, and the mid-autumn Moon Festival. Chinatown is a 10- to 15-minute cab ride from the Loop, and during summer weekends it's also accessible via a free trolley that departs from the Field Museum and from the intersection of State Street and Roosevelt Road. *Phone 312/326-5320 (Chinatown Chamber of Commerce). www.chicagochinatown.org.*

★ ★ ★ ★ EVEREST (MAP A)

440 S LaSalle St (60605)
Phone 312/663-8920
Fax 312/663-8802
www.leye.com

Perched high atop the city on the 40th floor of the Chicago Stock Exchange building, Everest affords spectacular views and equally fabulous contemporary French cuisine. Chef/owner Jean Joho blends European influences with local, seasonal American ingredients; he is not afraid to pair noble ingredients like caviar and foie gras with humbler fruits of American soil such as potatoes and turnips. The à la carte menu offers several signature dishes, including the Fantasy of Chocolate—five different riffs on the decadent cocoa theme artfully piled onto one glorious plate. Everest's dining room is luxuriously decorated with polished gold railings, vaulted draped ceilings, mirrored walls, and, of course, floor-to-ceiling windows for fabulous unobstructed views. *Secret Inspector's Notes: The view at Everest draws mostly heavy-hitters looking to impress clients or other important business contacts. This is for good reason, as everything about the restaurant is ideal for an important business meal, a romantic evening, or a special occasion. With the high-floor view of the city and formal setting, Everest is sure to wow young and old diners alike.* French menu. Dinner. Closed Sun-Mon; Jan 1, Dec 25. Bar. Reservations recommended. Valet parking. **$$$$**

★ ★ GIOCO (MAP A)

1312 S Wabash Ave (60605)
Phone 312/939-3870
Fax 312/939-3858
www.gioco-chicago.com

A riot of earthy flavors is in store at this chic former speakeasy in the South Loop. The simply sophisticated Italian food is offered up in a comfortable setting that's simultaneously rustic and clubby—and the seasonal outdoor patio is a rare treat in this up-and-coming neighborhood. Italian menu. Menu changes seasonally. Closed holidays. Lunch, dinner. Bar. Casual attire. **$$$**

★ ★ LA STRADA 7 (MAP A)

155 N Michigan Ave (60601)
Phone 312/565-2200
Fax 312/565-2216
www.lastradaristorante.com

If you're looking for La Strada at the corner of Michigan Avenue and Randolph Street in the Loop, look down: this elegant Italian restaurant sits below street level. But an atrium of windows allows light to flood in, revealing warm, wood-trimmed rooms and linen-topped tables with handsome appointments. Veal is the house specialty at La Strada, supplemented by beef, chicken, and fish main courses. Get friendly with the crowd over after-dinner drinks in the piano bar. Northern Italian menu. Lunch, dinner. Closed Sun; holidays. Bar. Valet parking. **$$$**

★ ★ NICK'S FISHMARKET (MAP A)
51 S Clark St (60603)
Phone 312/621-0200
Fax 312/621-1118
www.nicksfishmarketchicago.com
Although Nick's specializes in seafood, it acts in every other way like a steakhouse. Consider the dark, subterranean room with low ceilings and attentive tuxedoed waiters. Traditional preparations like lobster bisque and lobster thermador encourage the simile. But in the kitchen, Nick is all about fish. An operation born in Hawaii in the mid-1960s, Nick's reveals its roots in Hawaiian fish specials and the "Maui Wowie" salad. Appetizers feature shellfish, sashimi, and caviar, followed by sole, salmon, and lobster entrées. The street-level bar serves casual versions. American menu. Lunch, dinner. Closed Sun; holidays. Bar. Children's menu. Valet parking. **$$$**

state street, that great street

Yes, State Street is "that great street" alluded to in song. Once dubbed the busiest intersection in the world, State Street today is a Loop shopping mecca anchored by Chicago's two most famous department retailers, Marshall Field's and Carson Pirie Scott. These flagship stores have been joined by national chains, discount stores, and specialty shops. More interesting than the merchandise available for purchase, however, may be the street's architecture. Check out the graceful Louis Sullivan grillwork at Carson's main entrance, the Tiffany dome inside Field's, and the exterior of the Hotel Burnham, a masterful renovation and restoration of the former Reliance Building, once termed "the crown jewel of Chicago architecture." For lunch, try Marshall Field's venerable **Walnut Room** or the **Atwood Café** in the Hotel Burnham. And if you need to meet up with someone, do so under the Marshall Field's clock at Washington and State as Chicagoans have done for generations.

★ ★ ★ OPERA (MAP A)
1301 S Wabash Ave (60605)
Phone 312/461-0161
Helping to position the gentrifying South Loop as a foodie destination, Opera updates Chinese fare by banning gummy sauces and upping the presentation appeal. Top picks include five-spice squid and slow-roasted pork shoulder. The lively, art-filled interior—don't miss the Asian girlie collages—encourages lingering over cocktails. But romantics are served by tables set within a series of narrow vaults in this former film storage warehouse. Chinese menu. Dinner. Closed holidays. Bar. Casual attire. **$$$**

★ ★ ★ THE PALM (MAP A)
323 E Wacker Dr (60601)
Phone 312/616-1000
Fax 312/616-3717
www.thepalm.com
While some people feel that this classic concept has become watered down, The Palm in the Swissotel still delivers on its promise of giant steaks and lobsters in a business-casual steakhouse atmosphere, complete with a caricature wall of fame and platinum-card prices. Seasonal outdoor seating offers great views. American, steak menu. Lunch, dinner. Bar. Casual attire. Valet parking. Outdoor seating. **$$$**

★ ★ PETTERINO'S (11) (MAP A)
150 N Dearborn (60601)
Phone 312/422-0150
www.leye.com
Named after Arturo Petterino, the longtime maitre d' of Chicago's famed Pump Room, this theater-district restaurant packs in a crowd that loves the 1940s supper club feel. Classic Italian-American dishes like chicken cacciatore, spaghetti and meatballs, and veal marsala are served nightly in this darkly lit, wood-paneled dining room with welcoming red booths. Italian, American, steak menu. Closed Sun. Lunch, dinner. Bar. Valet parking. **$$**

★ ★ RUSSIAN TEA TIME (MAP A)
77 E Adams St (60603)
Phone 312/360-0000
Fax 312/360-0575
www.russianteatime.com
Despite the name, the emphasis here is on Russian food rather than tea. Traditional caviar service and classics like borscht, salmon blinis, and stuffed cabbage wave the old-world torch, as does the time-

warp look of red booths, brass chandeliers, and waiters in tuxedos.
Neighboring both the Art Institute of Chicago and Symphony Center,
Russian Tea Time draws a cultured crowd. Russian menu. Closed
holidays. Lunch, dinner. Bar. Casual attire. Outdoor seating. **$$**

★★ TRATTORIA NO. 10 (MAP A)
10 N Dearborn St (60602)
Phone 312/984-1718
Fax 312/984-1525
www.trattoriaten.com
A rustic yet elegant respite from the hectic rush of the Loop business
district, Trattoria No. 10 welcomes diners with arched ceilings, murals,
and ceramic tile floors. House-made ravioli is a specialty, as are
pastas, risottos, and fresh seafood selections on the menu of updated
Italian classics. A popular lunch and dinner spot for downtown
denizens, Trattoria No. 10 is perhaps best known for its bountiful,
bargain-priced cocktail hour buffet—a great pre-theater option or
pick-me-up after museums and shopping. Italian menu. Lunch, din-
ner. Closed Sun; holidays. Bar. Casual attire. Valet parking. **$$**

★★ VIVERE (14) (MAP A)
71 W Monroe St (60603)
Phone 312/332-4040
Fax 312/332-2656
www.italianvillage-chicago.com
The high end of a trio of restaurants that comprises the Loop's long-
standing Italian Village, Vivere plays it cool with showy décor and
luxurious meals. The warmly lit dining room with decorative scrolls
and swirls aims to distract, but the food stands its ground with riffs
on the familiar, such as squid ink tortellini stuffed with bass. The
Italian wine list rates among the country's best, making this a solid
special-occasion choice. Italian menu. Lunch, dinner. Closed Sun; holidays. Bar. Casual attire. Reservations recommended. Valet parking. **$$**

North Side

When it comes to restaurants, shopping, and nightlife, no area in Chicago can compete with the city's north side. From the mostly commercial Magnificent Mile to the more residential Lakeview neighborhood, Chicago's north side offers endless entertainment options and will appeal to anyone looking to have fun.

The near north side of Chicago, which encompasses the Gold Coast, River North, and Streeterville neighborhoods, is best explored on foot. Begin your trek at the Chicago River, crossing the waterway on the Michigan Avenue Bridge and Esplanade. Here, at the southern end of the Magnificent Mile, stand two of Chicago's most prominent and beautiful buildings: the Tribune Tower and the Wrigley Building. On the east side of Michigan Avenue, the Tribune Tower's Gothic design, ornately decorated with flying buttresses, was inspired by the Button Tower of the cathedral at Rouen, France. The base of the building is studded by stones from locations around the world, including all 50 states, the Parthenon, Taj Mahal, and the Pyramids of Egypt. Directly across the street, the Wrigley Building, modeled after the Seville Cathedral's Giralda Tower in Spain, features a cream-colored terra-cotta exterior and dramatic, four-dial clock tower rising 30 stories above street level.

Proceed down the crowded sidewalks of North Michigan Avenue, soaking up the vibrant atmosphere of the Magnificent Mile, a shopping mecca that draws visitors from around the world. Most of the major retailers—including Nordstrom, Neiman Marcus, and Bloomingdale's—have a presence here, as do upscale boutiques like Tiffany & Co and Giorgio Armani. At the north end of the "Mag Mile," the eight-story Water Tower Place shopping mall is anchored by Marshall Field's and Lord & Taylor. The mall's namesake, the historic Chicago Water Tower, still stands at 800 North Michigan Avenue, having survived the Great Chicago Fire of 1871, a calamity that destroyed the homes of 100,000 Chicagoans—one-third of the population at that time. Nearby, the John Hancock Center stretches 100 stories skyward, with an open-air observation deck on its 94th floor.

At the north end of the Magnificent Mile, just past the famous Drake Hotel, cross Lake Shore Drive and kick off your shoes as you stroll upon the sands of Oak Street Beach. During the summer months, Chicago's hippest beach fills up with tanned and beautiful bodies.

Just south of Oak Street Beach is Navy Pier, home to numerous restaurants and shops, as well as a botanical garden and an IMAX Theater. While visiting the 3,000-foot-long pier, you can even ride a 15-story Ferris wheel, a replica of the one used at the 1893 World's Fair in Chicago. In the summer, the city offers twice-weekly fireworks displays at Navy Pier.

Few driving experiences can compare with the thrill of cruising on North Lake Shore Drive on a warm, sunny day, windows rolled down, Chicago's beautiful skyline to the west, while, to the east, the expansive waters of Lake Michigan lead out into the distant horizon. North Lake Shore Drive also serves as an excellent way to access the north side's most popular neighborhoods, beginning with Lincoln Park. Here, you'll find 300 acres of parkland to explore, including a free zoo and conservatory. With its setting along the lakefront, Lincoln Park is a popular destination for joggers, bikers, and rollerbladers.

Venturing west of the lake, you'll discover residential areas cut up by narrow streets and tree-lined sidewalks, along with main arteries—such as Clark and Halsted streets—occupied by restaurants, coffee shops, boutiques, and clubs. A number of successful rock acts, including the Smashing Pumpkins, Liz Phair, and Wilco, launched their careers by performing at north side clubs like the Vic Theatre and the Aragon Ballroom. The area is populated mainly by the 30-and-under crowd, although you'll also find a number of empty nesters who chose to abandon suburban life once their children grew up and left home.

The Lakeview neighborhood is home to the Chicago Cubs and the team's charming, much-loved ballpark, Wrigley Field. The ballpark's ivy-covered walls and manual scoreboard offer fans a turn-back-the-clock experience every time they take in a game. Opened in 1914 as Weeghman Park, Wrigley Field became Cubs Park when chewing-gum magnate William Wrigley bought the team in 1920, only to change to its present name six years later. The "Friendly Confines," as Cubs fans call their home, last hosted a World Series in 1945, when the Cubs lost to the Detroit Tigers four games to three. The Cubs haven't won a World Series championship since 1908.

Restaurants on the North Side

★ A LA TURKA (MAP E)
3134 N Lincoln Ave (60657)
Phone 773/935-6101
Fax 773/935-8894
www.turkishkitchen.us
Belly dancing shows and sunken tables surrounded by pillow seats lend exotic allure to this north side Turkish eatery. Sharable starters are ideally suited to grazing. For a complete culinary journey, progress from bread spreads and salads to grilled meats, concluding with muddy Turkish coffee. Make like the Turks who frequent A La Turka and bring the late-night gang to its weekend dances. Turkish menu. Closed holidays. Dinner, late-night. Bar. Casual attire. Outdoor seating. **$**

★ ABU NAWAS (MAP B)
2411 N Clark St (60614)
Phone 773/529-1705
For good, cheap, and plentiful portions of savory Middle Eastern fare, it's hard to beat Abu Nawas. This cheerful, smoke-free Lincoln Parker serves heaping plates of hummus and the eggplant spread baba ghanoush with pita bread, falafel with mango sauce, and grilled lamb kebab skewers. Wash it down with juice, tea, a yogurt drink, or Turkish coffee (alcohol is BYOB). Its prime location near Clark and Fullerton streets makes Abu Nawas a great lunchtime shopping stop. Middle Eastern menu. Lunch, dinner. Casual attire. **$**

★ ★ ADOBO GRILL (MAP B)
1610 N Wells St (60614)
Phone 312/266-7999
Fax 312/266-9299
www.adobogrill.com
Fans of beyond-the-taco Mexican food will appreciate this upscale, up-tempo Old Towner known for its extensive tequila list, tableside guacamole preparation, and intriguing (and extensive) menu offerings—with some equally intriguing cocktails. The scene at night can be raucous; brunch-time is quieter. Mexican menu. Dinner, brunch. Closed holidays. Two vintage bars. Children's menu. Casual attire. Outdoor seating. **$$**

★ ★ ★ ★ AMBRIA   **18** (MAP B)

2300 N Lincoln Park W (60614)
Phone 773/472-5959
www.leye.com

Ambria is located at the base of Lincoln Park in The Belden-Stratford, a 1922 architectural landmark turned residential hotel on Chicago's romantic lakefront. With dark mahogany walls and luxuriously appointed tabletops set with tiny shaded votive lamps, this beautiful, graceful space is filled with radiant women and striking men who glow in the room's creamy amber light. Ambria is a civilized spot, ideal for business or pleasure. The menu is as elegant as the room, with Mediterranean accents from Italy, Spain, and beyond (saffron, piquillo peppers, olives, and polenta) turning up the flavor on the kitchen's top-quality selection of fish, game, lamb, and beef. In addition to the enticing à la carte menu, the kitchen offers the Ambria Classic menu, a decadent five-course prix fixe option that should be ordered if a big enough appetite presents itself. The service is helpful, efficient, and warm, making dining here a delight on every level. *Secret Inspector's Notes: The staff at Ambria is enjoyably warm and enthusiastic, making each decision throughout your meal an exercise in pleasure. Nervous about wine? The wine steward makes every diner feel comfortable during that decision-making process.* French menu. Menu changes seasonally; daily specialties. Closed Sun; holidays. Dinner. Bar. Jacket required. Reservations recommended. Valet parking. **$$$$**

★ ANN SATHER   **19** (MAP E)

929 W Belmont Ave (60657)
Phone 773/348-2378
Fax 773/348-1731
www.annsather.com

Open since 1945, this Swedish family of comfy, come-as-you-are restaurants may be best known for its sinful cinnamon rolls, but fans of all ages also appreciate the hearty Swedish and American classics (for example, Swedish pancakes with lingonberries, roast turkey dinner), the no-nonsense service, and the reasonable prices. The breakfast menu is available all day. Four additional locations can be found on the city's north side, at 5207 N Clark, 1448 N Milwaukee, 3416 N Southport, and 3411 N Broadway. Swedish, American menu. Breakfast, lunch, dinner. Bar. **$**

★★ ARCO DE CUCHILLEROS **20** (MAP C)
3445 N Halsted St (60657)
Phone 773/296-6046
Located in a storefront in the bustling Lakeview neighborhood, this charming eatery features more than 40 different selections of soups, hot and cold tapas, and larger entrées, as well as what has been said to be the best sangria in the city. Enjoy the authentic Spanish cuisine at one of the cozy tables tucked away in the dining room or, in warmer months, dine on the outdoor backyard patio, aglow with torches and candles. Spanish, tapas menu. Dinner, Sun brunch. Closed Mon; holidays. Bar. Casual attire. Outdoor seating. **$**

★★★ ATLANTIQUE **21** (MAP F)
5101 N Clark St (60640)
Phone 773/275-9191
Fax 773/275-9199
An Andersonville neighborhood joint with cooking worthy of a downtown address, Atlantique specializes in seafood. From the huge marlin over the bar to the starfish-shaped sconces, the décor plays up the menu motif. Chef/owner Jack Jones borrows from the culinary cultures of Asia, Italy, and France in dishes like panko-dusted crab cakes, warm lobster salad with truffle oil, and seared tuna au poivre. Oysters often turn up among specials, and landlubbers get interesting choices, too, such as venison and duck confit. Modern American, seafood menu. Dinner. Closed Mon. Bar. Casual attire. Reservations recommended. Outdoor seating. **$$$**

★★★ AVENUES **22** (MAP A)
108 E Superior (60611)
Phone 312/573-6754
chicago.peninsula.com
Set in an elegant space on the fifth floor of the Peninsula Hotel, Avenues offers creative contemporary fare with an emphasis on seafood, served by polished professionals in a refined ambience. The wine list is expertly chosen to harmonize with the food. Hushed tones and a discreet, old-world service attitude bespeak this modern restaurant's spot in the upper echelon of fine urban hotel dining. American, seafood, Asian menu. Breakfast, lunch, dinner. Bar. Business casual attire. **$$$$**

★★ BANDERA **23** (MAP A)
535 N Michigan Ave (60611)
Phone 312/644-3524
www.banderarestaurants.com
A shopper's delight one story above Michigan Avenue, Bandera

boosts its Mag Mile views with a crowd-pleasing American menu. The emphasis is on Western (think baby-back ribs) and rotisserie fare (spit-roasted chicken), but the restaurant offers enough variety on offer to please most tastes. Vintage photographs of Chicago localize this link in the Houston's restaurant chain. American menu. Closed Sun; Thanksgiving, Dec 25. Lunch, dinner. Bar. Children's menu. Casual attire. **$$**

from cultural to gastronomic melting pot

At the turn of the century they came—from Germany, Bohemia, Sweden, Ireland. Immigrant populations. Sometimes three generations of families, sometimes couples just beginning families, sometimes men without families. Most didn't speak the language. When they were able to get work, it was usually as unskilled laborers, and the hours were long and grueling.

A yearning for comfort was eased by living among people who knew their own culture. Thus, as in New York and other urban areas, ethnic neighborhoods began to emerge—German neighborhoods, Polish neighborhoods, Norwegian neighborhoods, Russian, Danish, Scottish, Italian, Chinese, Irish, Greek—neighborhoods that gave Chicago so much of its cultural diversity and still-thriving flavor. These areas created a cultural melting pot and, in due course, gave way to a gastronomic melting pot.

Lucky for Chicagoans—and visitors—the city's ethnic restaurants continue to thrive. From the city's main drags to its hidden side streets, restaurants with you-name-it cuisines await hungry adventurers. Ethiopian? Try **Ras Dashen** (5846 N Broadway), named for the highest mountain in Ethiopia. Its authenticity stems from its chef, who owned a restaurant in her home province of Gondar. Mediterranean? Try **Tizi Melloul**, at 531 N Wells—and then you can say that you've eaten at the namesake of a mountain in Morocco. Mexican? No mountain here, but **Salpicon** (1252 N Wells) will cheer you with authentic classic and contemporary dishes inspired by the chef's home in Mexico City. The Middle East? **Sayat Nova** (157 E Ohio) has been a Chicago favorite for 25 years.

If you have time, take a stroll through some of the city's best-known ethnic neighborhoods. Chicago's Greektown is an area running from Randolph to Van Buren (north to south) and Racine to Halsted (east to west), and the area's sights and sounds tantalize the senses. Stop at restaurants like **The Parthenon** (314 S Halsted), with its huge menu, said to be the oldest restaurant in Greektown; or check out the open kitchen at **Greek Islands** (200 S Halsted), Greektown's largest restaurant.

Some of the city's best Italian delights are found on West Taylor Street in an area called Little Italy. In between shops selling delectable Italian ice and other sweet treats is the popular **Rosebud** (1500 W Taylor St), where celebrity sightings are not uncommon, and **Tuscany** (1014 W Taylor St), serving rustic northern Italian fare.

In the Swedish area called Andersonville along Clark Street between Foster and Bryn Mawr, you can trace the experiences of Chicago's Swedish Americans at the Swedish American Museum Center (5211 N Clark St). Afterward, walk a few doors south to 5207 N Clark St to **Ann Sather** for potato sausage, Swedish pancakes, or the wildly popular cinnamon rolls. (You say cinnamon rolls didn't come from Sweden? Try them before you think of complaining.)

★ BASTA PASTA (MAP G)
6733 Olmstead St (60631)
Phone 773/763-0667
Fax 773/763-1114
www.bastapastachicago.com
Homemade Italian food like "mama" used to make is the order of the day at this restaurant, located in a former bank in the Edison Park neighborhood (the bathrooms are the former vaults). Favorites like spaghetti, linguini, and rigatoni are served in gargantuan portions that, when you're done eating, may feel as if they were the size of the giant bowl of pasta that marks the restaurant's exterior. But despite its name, pasta isn't the only reason to visit—the menu also offers a good selection home-style seafood and chicken dishes, pizzas, and salads. Italian menu. Lunch, dinner. Closed Mon. Bar. Children's menu. Casual attire. Outdoor seating. **$$**

★ BELLA DOMANI ② (MAP F)
4603 N Lincoln Ave (60625)
Phone 773/561-9177
Bella Domani specializes in traditional Italian meals in Lincoln Square, an area with a growing reputation for dining. The Lincoln Avenue

storefront covers its bases with steak, fish, and pasta dishes including classic Sicilian rice balls. Although the menu prices aren't cheap, most entrées come with soup, salad, and side that prove amply filling. Both area families and couples appreciate the restaurant's casual tone. Italian menu. Dinner. Closed Mon. Bar. Casual attire. **$$**
🅓

★ ★ ★ BICE 26 (MAP A)
158 E Ontario St (60611)
Phone 312/664-1474
Fax 312/664-9008
www.biceristorante.com
A chain that grew out of Milan, Bice stays true to its northern Italian roots at its Chicago link. The Art Deco-inspired design provides a glamorous backdrop in sync with the chic Streeterville neighborhood in which it resides. While the menu changes monthly, expect hits including veal Milanese and beef carpaccio. For a cheaper, more casual version of Bice food, try its sibling next door, Bice Café, a lunchtime favorite of Michigan Avenue shoppers. Northern Italian menu. Lunch, dinner. Closed Jan 1, Dec 25. Bar. Children's menu. Casual attire. Valet parking. Outdoor seating. **$$$**

★ ★ BIN 36 27 (MAP A)
339 N Dearborn St (60610)
Phone 312/755-9463
Fax 312/755-9410
www.bin36.com
This wine-centric River North restaurant and bar pairs 50 wines with moderately priced, creative American food. There's an environment for every occasion, from an after-work cocktail at the bar to a light bite in the lounge to a full meal in the dining room. A retail section sells wine and related goodies. American menu. Breakfast, lunch, dinner. Bar. Casual attire. **$$**

★ ★ BRASSERIE JO 28 (MAP A)
59 W Hubbard St (60610)
Phone 312/595-0800
Fax 312/595-0808
www.leye.com
In the brasserie tradition, Jean Joho's spacious, lively River North spot welcomes café society for a quick bite with a glass of moderately priced French wine or handcrafted beer, iced fruits de mer at the zinc bar, or a leisurely meal of robust, reasonably priced Alsatian-French fare. Menu classics include salad Niçoise, choucroute, coq au vin,

and bouillabaisse. Light floods in from the street-level windows; vast murals, woven café chairs, and tile floors create a chic, vintage Parisian atmosphere. To finish your meal, request a visit from the "cheese chariot." French bistro menu. Lunch, dinner. Closed Thanksgiving, Dec 24-25. Bar. Valet parking. Outdoor seating. **$$**

★ ★ BRETT'S 29 (MAP F)
2011 W Roscoe St (60618)
Phone 773/248-0999
Although Brett's is a popular spot for weekend brunch, the dim lighting, understated décor, and soft background music make it an ideal destination for a romantic dinner as well. But don't be afraid to bring the whole family—a children's menu offers the little ones a variety of pastas and sandwiches, and, although the dining experience is relatively upscale, the atmosphere remains casual. You can even bring along the family dog in good weather, when man's best friend is allowed at outdoor tables. American menu. Dinner, brunch. Closed Mon-Tues; holidays. Bar. Children's menu. Casual attire. Outdoor seating. **$$**

★ ★ BRICKS 30 (MAP B)
1909 N Lincoln Ave (60614)
Phone 312/255-0851
If you're craving gourmet pizza (and maybe a nice cold beer to accompany it), head to this restaurant and pub, a favorite with locals. Build your own pizza from a list of toppings that includes Maytag blue, gouda, and goat cheeses, banana peppers, and barbecue sauce, or enjoy one of Bricks' own creations, like the Ditka, a pizza tribute to the former Chicago Bears coach. An impressive selection of craft brews and imports is on hand, as are a number of wines by the glass, half-bottle, and bottle. Pizza. Dinner. Closed holidays. Bar. **$$**

★ ★ BUTTERFIELD 8 31 (MAP A)
711 N Wells St (60610)
Phone 312/327-0940
A see-and-be-seen River North hotspot, Butterfield 8 mingles the business of food with the pleasures of society. An underlit floor, high-backed booths, and bright colors set the stage for Butterfield's good-looking patrons. Despite its fashion-forwardness, the restaurant dares to revive culinary classics like steak tartare, oysters Rockefeller, shrimp de Jonghe, and veal schnitzel. Great people-watching and a long list of creative martinis serve to root you to your chair long after dessert. American menu. Dinner. Closed Sun. Bar. Casual attire. Outdoor seating. **$$**

★★ CAFE BA-BA-REEBA! 32 (MAP B)

2024 N Halsted St (60614)
Phone 773/935-5000
Fax 773/935-0660
www.cafebabareeba.com

The granddaddy of Chicago tapas spots, Cafe Ba-Ba-Reeba! was serving up those small plates long before "tapas" and "sangria" became household words. The colorful Mediterranean décor is the perfect complement to the lively Spanish cuisine. The authentic atmosphere is noisy and fun, and seating in the outdoor dining area is highly coveted in warm weather. You may find yourself waiting for a table, especially on weekends. Too hungry to wait? Take a seat at the front or back bar, where the full menu is available. Spanish, tapas menu. Lunch, dinner. Bar. Casual attire. Reservations recommended. Valet parking. Outdoor seating. **$$**

★★ CAFE BERNARD 33 (MAP B)

2100 N Halsted St (60614)
Phone 773/871-2100
www.cafebernard.com

If you're looking for a no-frills country French meal, you'll find it here. This intimate little café is sometimes overlooked for its flashier competition, but Café Bernard has been serving moderately priced fare in a cozy setting for more than 30 years. The kitchen offers dishes such as mussels, escargots, and steak au poivre that are simply, yet elegantly, presented. The menu is somewhat limited, but daily specials on the blackboard keep regulars returning. The low-lit, homey dining room, decorated with French posters, etchings, and dried flowers, serves as the perfect backdrop to the restaurant's cuisine and is a great spot for an intimate dinner for two. French menu. Dinner. Closed Dec 25. Bar. Casual attire. Outdoor seating. **$$**

★★ CAFE IBERICO 34 (MAP A)

739 N LaSalle Dr (60610)
Phone 312/573-1510
Fax 312/751-0098
www.cafe-iberico.com

Elbow your way into this River North tapas hotspot for small plates of hot and cold Spanish fare, refreshing sangria, and casual camaraderie. The food is great for sharing—whether in a group or on a date—and the atmosphere, while boisterous during prime time, creates a festive mood. Spanish, tapas menu. Lunch, dinner. Closed July 4, Thanksgiving, Dec 24-25. Bar. Casual attire. Outdoor seating. **$$**

★ ★ ★ CALITERRA **35** (MAP A)

633 N Saint Clair St (60611)
Phone 312/274-4444
Fax 312/274-0164
www.wyndham.com

Aptly named considering its Cal-Ital culinary concept (Tuscany meets northern California), this handsome—and somewhat hidden—oasis in the Wyndham Chicago Hotel draws a well-heeled Gold Coast business and shopping crowd. Innovative seasonal fare emphasizes organic produce and non-hormone-treated meats; additional monthly specialty menus showcase a particular ingredient in various preparations. The dining room is dressed in wood and textiles, with a display kitchen and a glass mural of a grape arbor as focal points. The gracious cocktail lounge, noteworthy cheese cart, and Italian-American wine list are additional highlights. Italian, California menu. Dinner. Children's menu. **$$$**

★ ★ CALLIOPE CAFE **36** (MAP E)

2826 N Lincoln Ave (60657)
Phone 773/528-8055

Lakeview's Calliope Café, popular with the neighborhood lunch crowd, distinguishes itself from the average deli with upscale sandwiches, splashes of colorful paint, and funky mismatched tables and chairs. Popular options include the salmon club, steak and avocado wrap, and pesto chicken sandwich, plus addictive homemade potato chips. You're unlikely to walk by this stretch of Lincoln Avenue, but the café offers an adjacent parking lot to encourage mealtime commuters. Deli menu. Lunch, dinner. Children's menu. Casual attire. Outdoor seating. **$**

★ ★ ★ CANTARE **37** (MAP A)

200 E Chestnut (60611)
Phone 312/266-4500

This upscale, sedate spot offers traditional Italian fare in a stylized Italianate setting. A few secluded booths line one wall, providing a romantic dining experience for a lucky few. This is white-tablecloth, Gold Coast dining—nothing too inventive, simply a hearty selection of steaks, veal, seafood, and pasta dishes, plus an enticing dessert cart. The bar is a nice place to take a shopping break or to wait for your date. Italian menu. Dinner. Bar. Casual attire. **$$**

lesser-known ethnic food festivals

Pick any summer weekend and you'll find happy, hungry Chicagoans eating and drinking their way through any number of the city's colorful food fairs. But Chicagoans know that the Grant Park festivals—big, bold, and fantastic—have crowds to match. So take a tip from the natives and try one of the city's smaller ethnic fests. Farther from the main drag, they have the color, the flavor, and, of course, the eats to make you say "yes!" in almost any language you choose.

- **A Taste of Polonia.** Chicago has the largest Polish community outside of Warsaw, and A Taste of Polonia, held each Labor Day weekend, gives witness. The biggest of the city's neighborhood festivals, it has had its share of famous visitors: the first President Bush, Dick Cheney, and Tipper Gore have all stopped in to eat kielbasa. Nonstop musical entertainment and Polish handicrafts provide something to do between nibbles. But as the Polish would say, *"Jedzcie, pijcie i popuszczajcie pasa,"* which means "Eat, drink, and loosen your belt." The festival is held on Lawrence and Milwaukee avenues Saturday through Monday.

- **Fiesta del Sol.** The Pilsen neighborhood has long been an area of home and hearth for Chicago's Mexican community. Fiesta del Sol is locally organized, most of the vendors are local, the profits support local schools, and each year the festival starts with a State of the Neighborhood address. The family atmosphere is both tobacco and alcohol free and is colorful and exuberant, with face-painting, Latin American music, Aztec drums, folklorica, mariachi bands, games, carnival and pony rides—and, of course, half a mile of the best tacos, enchiladas, tamales, gorditas, and other Mexican food this side of the border. You'll find it on Cermak Road between Morgan and Throop streets during the last weekend in July.

- **German Day.** Ask any previous visitor and the first thing they'll say about German Day is, "You must have a brat!" You can also have smoked sausage, potato salad, cakes, big, salty pretzels, and a host of other German delights, including beer tapped from a barrel on opening night. Saturday and Sunday bring singing and dancing performances by some of Chicago's German cultural societies. Carnival activities for the kids make this a family-friendly three days, held the weekend after Labor Day. The location is at the intersection of Lincoln, Leland, and Western avenues in Lincoln Square; look for the big tents.

- **Sorrento Cheese Festa Pasta Vino.** For four days over Father's Day weekend, the neighborhood around 24th Place and Oakley Avenue on Chicago's south side turns into ancient Rome. Roman columns, statues, and even the Trevi Fountain spring forth as the Sorrento Cheese Festa Pasta Vino brings music and dancing, Venetian costume parades, and kids' activities to life. But it's not called the Festa Pasta Vino for nothing; in addition to luscious offerings from neighborhood restaurants, a cooking stage makes your mouth water with every Italian delight imaginable. Come hungry; there is a cannoli-eating contest.

- **Osaka Garden Festival.** Chicago and Osaka are sister cities, and the relationship is celebrated with this cultural festival that highlights the arts and crafts, music, dance, and martial arts of Japan. The food, of course, is also celebrated—dig into a plate of yakisoba (hot noodles and vegetables with Japanese sauce, cooked on a griddle), tako-yaki (batter-grilled octopus nuggets with sauce), or chicken teriyaki and you'll see why. There are plenty of activities to keep the kids entertained, including kite-making, origami, and storytelling. This festival is held in Osaka Garden in Jackson Park on a mid-September weekend.

★★ CAPE COD ROOM   (MAP A)

140 E Walton Pl (60611)
Phone 312/440-8486; toll-free 800/553-7253
Fax 312/787-0256
www.thedrakehotel.com

Escape to a New England fishing town without leaving the city at this nautically themed seafood restaurant in the Drake Hotel. Decorated with dark wood walls, low-beamed ceilings, and red-and-white-checked tablecloths, the Cape Cod Room offers a comfortable place to dine—not to mention an extensive selection of seafood. From Dover sole and tuna to oysters and clams, seafood lovers will find everything their hearts desire here. Seafood menu. Lunch, dinner. Closed Dec 25. Bar. Casual attire. Valet parking. Outdoor seating.
$$$

★ ★ ★ THE CAPITAL GRILLE 39 (MAP A)
633 N Saint Clair St (60611)
Phone 312/337-9400
Fax 312/337-1259
www.thecapitalgrille.com
This Washington, DC-based chain deliberately cultivates the old boys' network vibe. The clubby, masculine décor features dark woods and original oil paintings of fox hunts, cattle drives, and the like. But even if cigars and cell phones aren't your thing, you'll find it hard to resist the top-notch steakhouse fare served up here. Sizable à la carte entrées like porterhouse steak, filet mignon, and broiled fresh lobster, along with traditional sides that serve three, tempt the taste buds and ensure that you'll leave feeling quite full. Beef is dry-aged on the premises for 14 days and hand-cut daily. The restaurant sits just off the Mag Mile in the same building that houses the Wyndham Chicago Hotel. Steak menu. Lunch, dinner. Closed July 4, Thanksgiving, Dec 25. Bar. Valet parking. **$$$**

★ ★ CARMINE'S 40 (MAP A)
1043 N Rush St (60611)
Phone 312/988-7676
Fax 312/988-7957
www.rosebudrestaurants.com
This Italian steak and seafood house, located in the ritzy Gold Coast area, has been a Chicago favorite since opening in 1995. Generously sized chops and steaks and hearty portions of seafood and pasta are served in the dim—and usually packed—dining room, where politicians, sports personalities, and celebrities have been known to turn up. Italian, seafood menu. Lunch, dinner, brunch. **$$**

★ ★ CERISE 41 (MAP A)
520 N Michigan Ave (60611)
Phone 312/327-0564
The fine dining room of the French-owned Le Meridien Chicago, Cerise hews to the hotel's nationality with a French menu. There are plenty of haut classics like foie gras and duck consommé, but the greatest applause here comes for the fish dishes and French comfort foods like chicken "gran mere." Finish with the chocolate and cherry crepes before heading next door to the convivial Le Rendezvous lounge for a digestif. French menu. Breakfast, lunch, dinner. Bar. Children's menu. Casual attire. Outdoor seating. **$$**

★ ★ ★ ★ ★ CHARLIE TROTTER'S 42 (MAP B)
816 W Armitage Ave (60614)
Phone 773/248-6228
Fax 773/248-6088
www.charlietrotters.com

Charlie Trotter's is a place for people who equate food with the highest form of art. It is also a restaurant for those who value a chef's masterful ability to transform sustenance into culinary wonder. But even those who doubt these two tenets will leave Charlie Trotter's understanding that food is not just for eating. It is for savoring, honoring, marveling at, and, most of all, thoroughly enjoying. Set inside a two-story brick brownstone, Charlie Trotter's is an intimate, peaceful temple of cuisine of the most refined and innovative variety. Trotter is the Nobel laureate of the kitchen—a mad maestro of gastronomy, if you will—and you must experience his talent for yourself to understand the hype. Charlie Trotter's offers several magnificent menus, including The Grand Tasting, The Vegetable Menu, and The Kitchen Table Degustation. Each combines pristine seasonal products (Trotter has a network of more than 90 purveyors, many of them local small farms) with impeccable French techniques and slight Asian influences. Trotter prefers saucing with vegetable juice-based vinaigrettes, light emulsified stocks, and purees as well as delicate broths and herb-infused meat and fish essences. The result is that flavors are remarkably intense, yet dishes stay light. Dining at Charlie Trotter's is an astonishing and extraordinary dining journey. *Secret Inspector's Notes: Don't worry if one of the menus doesn't appeal to your tastes; the staff will gladly take your preferences into consideration and customize your meal for you. The service couldn't be more gracious, warm, and inviting. Surprisingly, there is very little pretension here.* American menu with French and Asian influences. Dinner. Closed Sun-Mon; holidays. Jacket required. Reservations recommended. Valet parking. $$$$

★ ★ CHICAGO CHOP HOUSE 43 (MAP A)
60 W Ontario St (60610)
Phone 312/787-7100; toll-free 800/229-2356
Fax 312/787-3219
www.chicagochophouse.com

Choosing a steakhouse among the many in Chicago is no easy task, but independently owned Chicago Chop House stands out for its affinity for the metropolis. Papered in 1,400 photos of the city, its meat packers and mayors, most taken before 1930, the Chop House provides a history lesson as a side dish to meals centered on steaks and chops. Steak menu. Lunch, dinner. Closed holidays. Bar. Casual attire. Valet parking. Outdoor seating. $$$

★ CHICAGO DINER 44 (MAP C)
3411 N Halsted St (60657)
Phone 773/935-6696
www.veggiediner.com

If you think that vegetarian cuisine is nothing but lettuce leaves and sprouts, think again. Since 1983, this Lakeview diner has been serving hearty meatless fare that has won over the taste buds of vegetarians and meat lovers alike. Craving a hot dog? Try the "No Dog." How about Mexican food? They offer a "No Meata Fajita." Using products like seitan (wheat gluten), tofu (soybean curd), and tempeh (fermented soybean cake) along with grains, beans, and fresh vegetables, the Chicago Diner creates healthy alternatives to traditional meat dishes. A second location has opened in Highland Park, at 581 Elm Pl. Vegetarian menu. Lunch, dinner. Closed Jan 1, Dec 25. Bar. Casual attire. **$**

★★ CHILPANCINGO 45 (MAP D)
358 W Ontario St (60610)
Phone 312/266-9525
Fax 312/266-6428

Chef Geno Bahena cooked at Frontera Grill before breaking out on his own with Ixcapuzalco in Logan Square and the follow-up Chilpancingo downtown. Festooned in colorful folk art and murals, Chilpancingo creates a lively setting where authentic Mexican market fare, including quail and rabbit, merge with more familiar standards such as enchiladas and ceviche on the menu. Mexican menu. Lunch, dinner. Closed Jan 1, Dec 25. Bar. Casual attire. **$$**

★★ COCO PAZZO 46 (MAP A)
300 W Hubbard St (60610)
Phone 312/836-0900
Fax 312/836-0257

A renovated loft with velvet swagged curtains and rustic wood floors sets an aptly dramatic stage for the robust Italian cooking on offer at Coco Pazzo. Chef Tony Priolo mans the stoves, turning out recipes that range from the sophisticated but uncomplicated beef carpaccio with black truffle oil to the crowd-pleasing rigatoni with sausage and cream. Pastas come in appetizer portions, allowing you to save room for the traditional Italian "second plate" of Florentine steak or wood-fired salmon. A longtime River North resident, Coco Pazzo draws dealmakers among the ad and art world types working nearby. Italian menu. Lunch, dinner. Closed Thanksgiving, Dec 25. Bar. Casual attire. Valet parking. Outdoor seating. **$$**

★ ★ ★ COOBAH (MAP F)
3423 N Southport Ave (60657)
Phone 773/528-2220

Latin eats and lots of drinks make hip Coobah a restaurant that crosses over into a late-night hangout. The kitchen puts in long hours, beginning with a creative weekend brunch that includes a Spanish-style granola and chorizo gravy with biscuits, plus sandwiches such as the Cuban reuben. Dinner is the main event; you can get it until 1 am nightly, 2 am on Saturday. Tamales, lamb adobo, and fish with Spanish olives testify to the range of dishes offered here. Freely flowing mojitos, sangria, and "Coobah libres" encourage diners to stick around this swinging Southport stop. Latin American menu. Breakfast, lunch, dinner, late-night. Bar. Casual attire. Outdoor seating. **$$**

★ ★ ★ ★ CROFTON ON WELLS (MAP A)
535 N Wells St (60610)
Phone 312/755-1790
Fax 312/755-1890
www.croftononwells.com

Suzy Crofton's acclaimed American cuisine is served in simply stylish, neutral-chic surroundings in this River North storefront. Expect a gracious, grown-up dining experience; the quiet, understated room and absence of "scene" diminish distractions from what's on your plate. Seasonal ingredients star on classically trained Crofton's limited menu of sophisticated regional cuisine, which features bold and earthy undertones. The carefully selected, reasonably priced wine list offers perfect pairings for the menu's attractions. American menu. Dinner. Closed Sun; holidays. Bar. Valet parking. **$$$**

★ ★ CYRANO'S BISTROT AND WINE BAR ⁴⁹ (MAP A)
546 N Wells St (60610)
Phone 312/467-0546
Fax 312/467-1850
www.cyranosbistrot.com

Cozy and unpretentious, Cyrano's is a country French getaway in Chicago's frenzied River North area. The rustic, un-Americanized menu encompasses bistro classics (including game and offal dishes), with a specialty in rotisserie meats. The décor is all sunny yellow walls, gilded mirrors, and provincial French accoutrements. The regional French wine list and bargain four-course lunch are added attractions, and an outdoor café makes diners part of the neighborhood scene in warm weather. Live cabaret and jazz entertainment is featured Fridays and Saturdays. French menu. Lunch, dinner. Closed Sun-Mon; July 4, Thanksgiving. Bar. Casual attire. Outdoor seating. **$$**

★ ★ ★ ★ THE DINING ROOM (MAP A)

160 E Pearson St (60611)
Phone 312/266-1000
Fax 312/266-1194
www.fourseasons.com

Innovative contemporary French cuisine is served in quiet luxury at The Dining Room, the opulent restaurant of The Ritz-Carlton. The décor of this striking, clubby room is rich and luxurious, from the fabrics to the breathtaking fresh flowers updated weekly. In addition to the superb à la carte choices—a signature dish is a succulent Maine lobster served with wild mushrooms over a crisp golden lobster cake—the chef offers an adventurous, personalized eight-course tasting menu, a five-course degustation menu, and a five-course vegetarian menu. To complement the fantastic fare, the award-winning wine list emphasizes boutique wines from Bordeaux, Burgundy, and California. The service at The Dining Room is in keeping with the décor. Waiters are tuxedoed and formal, and each presentation detail matches the classic atmosphere that the dining room strives to represent. *Secret Inspector's Notes: The Dining Room is an excuse for decadence. For a true culinary splurge, enjoy the Sunday brunch, a spread like no other. At dinner, the twice-baked potato with truffles is a starch lover's fantasy, and desserts created by award-winning pastry chefs surprise the sweet tooth in everyone.* French menu. Dinner, Sun brunch. Closed Mon. Children's menu. Reservations recommended. Valet parking. **$$$**

★ ★ DINOTTO RISTORANTE ⑤1 (MAP B)

215 W North Ave (60610)
Phone 312/202-0302

Dinotto endears itself to Old Town residents and tourists passing through alike with caring service, a warm atmosphere, and substantial, rustic Italian fare. Chili-spiced grilled calamari and goat cheese ravioli rank among the standouts on the menu, which offers plenty of chicken and veal options to succeed its pastas. In addition to the bustling dining room, seating spills onto a charming brick-walled outdoor patio in season. Italian menu. Lunch, dinner. Bar. Casual attire. Outdoor seating. **$$**

★ ED DEBEVIC'S ⑤2 (MAP A)

640 N Wells St (60610)
Phone 312/664-1707
Fax 312/664-7444
www.eddebevics.com

Treat your tweens and teens to Ed Debevic's, a retro 1950s diner where sassy, gum-snapping servers in period uniforms delight in giving diners

the classic chicago steakhouses

In the mid-1800s, on Chicago's south side from Pershing Avenue to 47th Street and from Halsted over to Ashland, there stood 320 acres of swampland that no one dreamed would one day help to put Chicago on the map. But the country's railways were expanding westward. The city was experiencing an influx of meat packers and livestock that its 48 scattered little stockyards couldn't handle. At the same time, the Civil War was raging, and the Mississippi River blockade had closed the north-south river trade route. So nine of the city's railroads banded together to purchase the swampy acreage. And on Christmas Day 1865, Chicago's Union Stock Yard and Transit Company officially opened, Chicago's famous stockyards were born, and no one has been able to separate Chicago from a flavorful slab of steak ever since.

This isn't to say the city hasn't been at the forefront of the culinary scene with other delights, putting forth menus that are either trendsetting or just plain high-quality. From Charlie Trotter's world-renowned oasis of dining and service to Gino's magnum opus of deep-dish pizza to Rich Melman and Lettuce Entertain You's popularization of the salad bar, Chicago has been a mecca of culinary creativity and high standards. But meat and potatoes? The decades-old mainstays are still around, still thriving, and still well loved. If you crave a good steak, Chicago has always been—and most definitely still is—your kind of town. Here are just a few of the still-thriving classics:

• **Eli's The Place for Steak:** The traditional steakhouse is alive and well and living just off Michigan Avenue. Eli Schulman, in the restaurant business since 1940, when he founded Eli's Ogden Huddle, opened his steak joint in the 1960s and was soon playing host to celebrities like Frank Sinatra and Liza Minelli. Large portions of prime beef are served in a dark wood and forest green atmosphere that feels like a throwback to a different time and place. The steakhouse concept doesn't get much clubbier than this.

• **Gene & Georgetti:** They say you can't lose with a Gene & Georgetti filet or 32-ounce T-bone. Is that why 56 members of the San Francisco Giants have eaten here? A lot of others have frequented this steakhouse, said to be Chicago's first. Locals, businesspeople, out-of-towners, and celebrities alike—Lee Iacocca loves it, Jackie Mason comes here, and

Sinatra is said to have come to Gene & Georgetti's straight from the airport (hmm…is a pattern of Frank and steakhouses developing here?). The atmosphere is dark, steakhouse classic, and cozy.

- **Lawry's The Prime Rib:** The first Lawry's The Prime Rib opened in California in 1938 and was meant to be elegant but not intimidating, with beef served tableside on silver carts. Chicago was its second location. Prime rib and Yorkshire pudding are the specialties here, and the silver carts are still very much in evidence. Lawry's has been in this space, formerly a puppet-opera theater, since 1974, and the atmosphere is lighter than the classic steakhouse. Booths fill the many dining rooms. And in case you're wondering, the famous seasoned salt was invented in the owner's kitchen especially for his restaurants' beef.

- **Morton's of Chicago:** Arnie Morton is a Chicago icon. Known for opening sometimes classic, sometimes trendy, but always high-quality Chicago restaurants—and now coast-to-coast concepts like this one—the original Morton's of Chicago is thriving in a below-street location that locals frequent when they want a large (okay, huge) slab of steak. Arnie has political connections, so politicians as well as celebrities are frequently found making deals within the restaurant's brick walls.

At any of these classic steak joints, you will know why author Edna Ferber commented that roast beef—though she might have been commenting on any kind of beef—"is not just a food. It is a philosophy."

a hard time. It's all in good fun, as is the lighthearted menu of burgers, hot dogs, and shakes, plus hearty Middle American staples like meat loaf and pot roast. American menu. Lunch, dinner. Closed Thanksgiving, Dec 24-25. Bar. Children's menu. Casual attire. Valet parking. **$**

★ ★ **ELI'S THE PLACE FOR STEAK** **(MAP A)**
215 E Chicago Ave (60611)
Phone 312/642-1393
Fax 312/642-4089
www.eliplaceforsteak.com
When Chicagoans hear the name Eli's, one thing comes to mind: cheesecake. But Eli's The Place for Steak was around long before the

now-famous dessert was; the late Eli Schulman opened his restaurant in 1966, and his cheesecake made its debut in 1980. Over the years, the restaurant has attracted many famous faces, from Frank Sinatra and Sean Connery to Chicago politicians and sports figures, and has also expanded its menu. No longer just "the place for steak," it's also the place for chops, seafood, and "Liver Eli." Steak menu. Lunch, dinner. Closed holidays. Bar. Children's menu. Casual attire. Valet parking. **$$**

★★★ ERAWAN   54 (MAP A)

729 N Clark St (60611)
Phone 312/642-6888

Far above the run-of-the-mill corner Thai spot, this fine-dining upstart follows the example of the famed Arun's (see) in upping the Thai ante with its menu, presentations, and prices. Contemporary, sometimes westernized versions of classic dishes are elaborately plated with carved vegetables and other decorative flourishes; there's even a seasonal degustation menu. The stylish setting, luxury table appointments, and soft-spoken service remind you that you're on a different sort of Thai dining adventure. The well-chosen wine list complements the food nicely. Thai menu. Lunch, dinner. Bar. Casual attire. Reservations recommended. **$$$$**

★★ ERWIN   55 (MAP B)

2925 N Halsted St (60657)
Phone 773/528-7200
Fax 773/528-1931
www.erwincafe.com

Low on contrivance, high on flavor, chef/owner Erwin Dreschler's "urban heartland" cuisine is right at home in his comfy and convivial north side restaurant. This is the thinking man's contemporary American comfort food, served amid a nature-inspired scheme of warm woods, forest green walls, and white tablecloths. The well-chosen wines, including extensive by-the-glass options, are central to the concept of the ever-changing seasonal menu (Dreschler is a champion of local foodstuffs and leads tours of area farmers' markets). With choices like banana-cinnamon French toast, eggs Benedict, and rainbow trout, erwin is also a popular brunch destination. American menu. Dinner, Sun brunch. Closed Mon; holidays. Bar. Valet parking. **$$**

★★ FINESTRA DI CALO (MAP F)

5341 N Clark St (60640)
Phone 773/334-4525

An upscale spin-off of the longstanding Italian restaurant Calo next door, Finestra takes aim at Andersonville's more youthful residents with contemporary décor, including floor-to-ceiling front windows that open completely onto Clark Street in summer. Although Finestra has experimented with modernized Italian food, it relies on Calo staples, including pizzas, ribs, and red-sauced pastas. Italian menu. Dinner. Closed Mon. Bar. Casual attire. **$$**

★★ FOGO DE CHÃO ⑤⑦ (MAP A)

661 N LaSalle St (60610)
Phone 312/932-9330
www.fogodechao.com

If you're in a carnivorous mood, this upscale, aromatic Brazilian churrascaria is the place to indulge. Fifteen all-you-can-eat grilled and roasted meats waft through the room on spits, borne by efficient "gauchos" who descend upon you at your whim. The massive salad bar and side dishes represent the other food groups—but at this price, save room for plenty of meat. Brazilian steakhouse menu. Lunch, dinner. Bar. Casual attire. **$$$**

★★ FRONTERA GRILL ⑤⑧ (MAP A)

445 N Clark St (60610)
Phone 312/661-1434
Fax 312/661-1830
www.fronterakitchens.com

Born of chef/owner Rick Bayless' genius for, and scholarly pursuit of, regional Mexican cuisine, this River North superstar's brand has become a name to reckon with. The casual, more accessible of Bayless' side-by-side duo (see also TOPOLOBAMPO), Frontera introduces a wealth of deceptively simple Mexican dishes—and a world of flavors—that you won't find at your neighborhood taco stand. An exhaustive tequila list for sipping or for shaken-to-order margaritas and a fine wine list stand up to the food. A seat here is a coveted one, as reservations are for parties of five to ten only. Mexican menu. Lunch, dinner, Sat brunch. Closed Sun-Mon; holidays. Bar. Children's menu. Casual attire. Valet parking. Outdoor seating. **$$**

★★ GEJA'S CAFE (MAP B)

340 W Armitage Ave (60614)
Phone 773/281-9101
Fax 773/281-0849
www.gejascafe.com

The fondue craze never ended at this venerable Lincoln Park classic, always at or near the top of all those "most romantic" lists. It's dark and cozy inside, and after all, there is something flirtatious about swirling your food around in a pot and occasionally crossing forks with your tablemate to the stylings of live flamenco guitar music. Fondue menu. Dinner. Closed holidays. Bar. Casual attire. **$$$**
D̪

★★★ GENE & GEORGETTI (MAP A)

500 N Franklin St (60610)
Phone 312/527-3718
Fax 312/527-2039
www.geneandgeorgetti.com

A veteran steakhouse with a masculine, insider's ambience and a past (it opened in 1941, long before River North was a hip 'hood), Gene & Georgetti is an old-school Chicago carnivore's haunt. Prime steaks, gigantic "garbage salad," and gruff service are among the draws. Italian, American menu. Lunch, dinner. Closed Sun; holidays; also the first week in July. Bar. Casual attire. Valet parking. **$$$**

★★★ GIBSON'S STEAKHOUSE ⑥¹ (MAP A)

1028 N Rush St (60611)
Phone 312/266-8999
Fax 312/787-5649
www.gibsonssteakhouse.com

The theme at Gibson's is outsized, from the massive steaks on the plate to the stogie-puffing personalities—a blend of politicians, sports figures, celebrities, and conventioneers—who energize the room. Carnivores crave the generous porterhouses here, but the kitchen also manages to issue some of the sea's biggest lobster tails and desserts that easily feed a four-top. Do call for a reservation, but don't be surprised if you still have to wait. In that case, squeeze into the smoky, convivial bar, order a martini, and prepare to make new friends. Steak, seafood menu. Lunch, dinner. Closed Easter, Thanksgiving, Dec 24-25. Bar. Casual attire. Valet parking. **$$$**

★★ HARRY CARAY'S 62 (MAP A)

33 W Kinzie St (60610)
Phone 312/828-0966
Fax 312/828-0962
www.hcrestaurantgroup.com

Although the legendary Cubs announcer died in 1998, his boisterous spirit thrives at this restaurant in River North, a vintage brick building emblazoned with Caray's signature expression, "Holy cow!" Inside, choose from the casual saloon with numerous sports-tuned TVs or the white-tablecloth dining room specializing in Harry's favorite food, Italian. Wherever you sit, you'll find a casual vibe and walls plastered with baseball memorabilia. Steak menu. Lunch, dinner. Closed Jan 1, Thanksgiving, Dec 25. Bar. Children's menu. Casual attire. Valet parking. **$$**

★★ HATSUHANA 63 (MAP A)

160 E Ontario St (60611)
Phone 312/280-8808
Fax 312/280-4545
www.hatsuhana.com

Located just off the busy Magnificent Mile, Hatsuhana attracts not only a number of tourists and travelers, but also locals who are hardcore sushi lovers. Serving fresh, high-quality sushi and sashimi is priority #1 at this elegant restaurant, where tuna, salmon, crab, octopus, clam, and other delicacies are offered both for lunch and dinner along with other items such as miso soup, tempura, and edamame. Sushi menu. Lunch, dinner. Closed Sun; holidays. Casual attire. Outdoor seating. **$$**

★★★ HEAT 64 (MAP B)

1507 N Sedgwick (60610)
Phone 312/397-9818; toll-free 866/230-6387
www.heatsushi.com

Top-tier, ultra-fresh sushi—some of which is still swimming in tanks under the bar—is the draw at this upscale spot in an up-and-coming stretch of Old Town. The menu changes daily, with occasional esoteric offerings that have earned Heat a loyal following of sushi purists. The multi-course, prix fixe omakase and kaiseki menus are beautifully presented culinary adventures. The minimal modern décor, gracious service, and fine selections of sake and wine complete the elevated experience. Japanese, sushi menu. Lunch, dinner. Closed Sun. Bar. Casual attire. **$$$$**

★★ HEAVEN ON SEVEN ON RUSH (MAP A)

600 N Michigan Ave (60611)
Phone 312/280-7774
www.heavenonseven.com

Chef Jimmy Bannos is Chicago's answer to New Orleans, cooking up Cajun and Creole dishes in this just-off-Michigan Avenue outpost. Cop a spot under the shelved hot sauce collection known as the Wall of Fire and order up red beans and rice, gumbo, and po' boy sandwiches. In addition to such standards, the dinner menu elaborates on the theme with gussied-up entrées like grilled salmon on andouille sausage and a multi-course tasting menu. Cajun/Creole menu. Lunch, dinner. Bar. Casual attire. $$

★ HEMA'S KITCHEN (MAP G)

6406 N Oakley Ave (60645)
Phone 773/338-1627

A small, intimate room with about ten tables is what makes up Hema's Kitchen. Chef Hema Potla runs this no-frills restaurant off the main Devon Avenue drag, where diners can choose from plenty of delicious and inexpensive traditional Indian dishes. You'll probably see Hema herself circling the room as she makes menu suggestions to her customers. But be forewarned—because of the restaurant's small size and its growing popularity, you may have to wait a while for a table. Indian menu. Lunch, dinner. Casual attire. $

★★ INDIAN GARDEN (MAP G)

2546 W Devon Ave (60659)
Phone 773/338-2929
Fax 773/338-3930
www.theindiangarden.com

A trip to the strip of Devon Street's Little India is worth the ride for lovers of Indian food. This classic is more upscale than some, with a bright interior and the requisite aromatic ambience. The generous buffet is a great deal, and there are plenty of vegetarian offerings. Indian menu. Buffet, lunch, dinner. Bar. Casual attire. Reservations recommended. $$

★★★ JAPONAIS (MAP D)

600 W Chicago Ave (60610)
Phone 312/822-9600
www.japonaischicago.com

This spacious River West restaurant is a sensuous, hip setting for contemporary Japanese fare that includes, but goes far beyond, traditional sushi. The creative menu inspires sharing and ordering in phases while enjoying the exotic cocktails or selections from the extensive sake and wine lists. Four dazzling environments set different moods; in warm weather, the subterranean riverfront terrace is an exotic escape. Contemporary Japanese, sushi menu. Lunch, dinner. Bar. Casual attire. Reservations recommended. Outdoor seating. **$$$**

★ ★ JIN JU 69 (MAP F)
5203 N Clark St (60640)
Phone 773/334-6377
Korean food gets the hipster treatment at Jin Ju. What emerges is a polished neighborhood ethnic with enough flair to entice newcomers to the exotic fare. By juicing the scene with techno beats and sleek décor, the Andersonville restaurant boosts the atmosphere missing at most Korean barbecue eateries. Despite the Western trappings, the food remains fairly traditional, including bi bim bop, kimchee soup, and barbecued short ribs. Don't miss the martinis made with the Korean liquor soju. Korean menu. Dinner. Closed Mon. Bar. Casual attire. **$$**

★ JOE'S BE-BOP CAFE 70 (MAP A)
700 E Grand Ave (60611)
Phone 312/595-5299
Fax 312/832-6986
www.joesbebop.com
On tourist-centric Navy Pier, Joe's unites two Chicago favorites, ribs and jazz. Cajun jambalaya and lighter salads supplement the tangy, slow-cooked ribs on the menu. Entertainment runs the jazz gamut from swing to Latin, with acts performing atop a raised stage that ensures good sightlines from around the expansive restaurant. Sunday brunch serves up a Bloody Mary bar and a big band. Barbecue menu. Lunch, dinner, Sun brunch. Closed Thanksgiving, Dec 25. Bar. Children's menu. Casual attire. Valet parking. Outdoor seating. **$$**

★ JOHN'S PLACE 71 (MAP E)
1202 W Webster Ave (60614)
Phone 773/525-6670
A solid neighborhood café in an unlikely residential locale—at the corner of Racine and Webster in the DePaul University area—guarantees John's a steady clientele. The food is comforting but conscientious. John's touts organic produce and line-caught fish in a menu that includes roast chicken, baked whitefish, and several vegetarian options. Families in particular crowd John's; expect to climb over strollers at lunch and the popular weekend brunch. American menu. Lunch, dinner, brunch. Closed Mon. Children's menu. **$$**

★ ★ ★ KEEFER'S   72 (MAP A)
20 W Kinzie (60610)
Phone 312/467-9525
www.keefersrestaurant.com
In bustling River North, stylish Keefer's offers prime steaks, chops,
seafood, and some bistro dishes served up in a handsome round
dining room with a contemporary Arts and Crafts feel. Soups, salads,
and sides are predominantly steakhouse classics (lobster bisque,
Caesar salad, creamed spinach), along with some updated but not
fussy alternatives. They also serve a somewhat pared-down lunch
menu, plus there's the adjacent "Keefer's Kaffe" with a menu of soups,
salads, and simple sandwiches, great for quick take-out. Steak menu.
Lunch, dinner. Closed Sun. Bar. Casual attire. Outdoor seating. **$$$**

★ ★ ★ KEVIN   73 (MAP A)
9 W Hubbard (60610)
Phone 312/595-0055
www.kevinrestaurant.com
Chicago fans of chef Kevin Shikami chased him from kitchen
to kitchen around town for years. But in Kevin, his eponymous
restaurant, they finally know where to find the talented chef each
night. From delicate fish to juicy meats, Shikami brings an Asian flair
to contemporary dishes that include tuna tartare, sesame-crusted
opakapaka (a Hawaiian fish), and sautéed buffalo strip steak. The
smart but warm River North room and polished servers make Kevin a
good choice for shoppers and business lunches, too. American, French,
Asian menu. Lunch, dinner. Closed Sun. Bar. Outdoor seating. **$$$**

★ ★ ★ KIKI'S BISTRO   74 (MAP A)
900 N Franklin St (60610)
Phone 312/335-5454
Fax 312/335-0614
Long before bistros were blossoming all over town, this little charmer
on an out-of-the-way corner in River North was pleasing patrons
with its traditional bistro fare and regional specials. The softly lit dining rooms are appointed in wood, rose-pink draping and upholstery,
and lace curtains. A somewhat older crowd frequents cozy, casual
Kiki's for its romantic, country inn ambience, reliable kitchen, and free
valet parking (a real boon in this bustling neighborhood). It's also fun
to dine at the bar here. French bistro menu. Lunch, dinner. Closed
Sun; holidays. Bar. Casual attire. **$$**

★★KLAY OVEN (MAP D)
414 N Orleans St (60610)
Phone 312/527-3999
Fax 312/527-1563
www.klayoven.com

White tablecloths, exotic textiles, and tasteful serving carts set the tone for fine Indian dining at Klay Oven. Offerings include several tandoori options, plenty of vegetarian choices, and eight varieties of fresh-baked bread. Wine and beer options exceed expectations, and the lunch buffet is a great deal for the quality. Indian menu. Lunch, dinner. Closed holidays. Bar. Casual attire. Outdoor seating. **$$**

★★LA BOCCA DELLA VERITA 76 (MAP F)
4618 N Lincoln Ave (60618)
Phone 773/784-6222
Fax 773/784-6272
www.laboccachicago.com

Lincoln Square's longstanding Italian storefront La Bocca Della Verita was here and popular before the neighborhood took off (witness the restaurant's wall of fame featuring old headshots of past stars who have dined here). Ample portions of well-priced northern Italian dishes cooked with the flair of a downtown café bring guests back for more. Raves go to the duck breast ravioli and sea bass baked in salt. Neighboring the Davis Theatre, Bocca makes a great pre- or post-movie dinner date. Italian menu. Lunch, dinner. Closed Mon; holidays. Casual attire. Outdoor seating. **$$**

★LA CREPERIE 77 (MAP B)
2845 N Clark St (60657)
Phone 773/528-9050

A Clark Street staple since 1971, La Creperie is Chicago's sole source for eat-out French crepes. Everything from coq au vin to curry gets wrapped in thin, pastry-style pancakes. That goes for dessert, too: the options here include the classic flaming crepes Suzette. French posters and candlelight create café romance in the storefront locale. French bistro menu. Breakfast, lunch, dinner. Closed Mon. Bar. Casual attire. Outdoor seating. **$$**

★★LA TACHE 78 (MAP F)
1475 W Balmoral Ave (60640)
Phone 773/334-7168

La Tache—French for "the spot"—looks and eats like a downtown restaurant. But to the good fortune of North Siders, it's located in Andersonville and priced accordingly. The smart French bistro offers comforting classics like sautéed escargot, duck à l'orange, and steak frites with enough creative spin to pique your palate. The service is far more professional than you'd expect in a neighborhood joint, and the owners invested La Tache with warm good looks courtesy of wood paneling and ceiling-suspended lamp shades. The busy bar traffics in wine and appetizers. French menu. Lunch, dinner, late-night. Bar. Casual attire. Outdoor seating. **$$**

★★ LAWRY'S THE PRIME RIB (MAP A)

100 E Ontario St (60611)
Phone 312/787-5000
Fax 312/787-1264
www.lawrysonline.com

As the name suggests, prime rib is the star at Lawry's The Prime Rib. At this unpretentious dining spot, it is offered in a variety of cuts for different tastes and appetites, from the smaller California cut to the extra-thick "Diamond Jim Brady" cut. Housed in the 1896 English manor-style McCormick Mansion, the restaurant exudes a stately feel, with hardwood furnishings, opulent chandeliers, a grand staircase, and a pair of brass lions outside the main dining area. Steak menu. Lunch, dinner. Closed Dec 25. Bar. Casual attire. Valet parking. **$$$**

★★ LE COLONIAL (MAP A)

937 N Rush St (60611)
Phone 312/255-0088
www.lecolonialchicago.com

While other, more daring Asian fusion concepts have come along, this Gold Coast link in an upscale chain holds its own with refined Vietnamese cuisine and elegant, escapist décor circa French-colonial Vietnam. This is a great place for a date or a Mag Mile shopping break. In warm weather, try to snag one of the much-coveted second-floor terrace tables. Vietnamese menu. Lunch, dinner. Bar. Outdoor seating. **$$**

★★★★ LES NOMADES ⑧¹ (MAP A)

222 E Ontario St (60611)
Phone 312/649-9010
Fax 312/649-0608
www.lesnomades.net

Les Nomades is a serene little spot tucked away from the bustle of Michigan Avenue in an elegant turn-of-the-century townhouse. Romantic and intimate, with a fireplace; hardwood floors; deep, cozy banquettes; and gorgeous flower arrangements, Les Nomades was originally opened as a private club. It is now open to the public, and what a lucky public we are. While many of Chicago's hottest dining rooms are filled with as much noise as they are with wonderful food, Les Nomades is a peaceful, reserved restaurant that offers perfect service and a magnificent menu of French fare flecked with Asian accents. Excessive noise is not present to distract you from the task at hand. Any spontaneous exclamations of love directed toward the delicious dishes you are consuming (game, foie gras, scallops, lamb, and fish among them) should be kept to a quiet roar, as the tables are closely spaced and exclamations of wonder are often shared. Dining here is a wonderful gastronomic experience, thus this is not a place for a casual dinner. Men are required to dine in jackets and ties, and women are comparably fitted for the occasion. Even children who are rightfully pampered by the attentive staff dress in their holiday best for a memorable evening. *Secret Inspector's Notes: This is a truly special place. After dining, you feel like you've been let in on a magnificently kept secret. It's a wonder to find such artful charm and atmosphere under one small roof.* French menu. Dinner. Closed Sun-Mon; holidays. Bar. Jacket required. Valet parking. **$$$$**

★ MAGGIANO'S LITTLE ITALY (MAP A)
516 N Clark St (60610)
Phone 312/644-7700
Fax 312/644-1077
www.maggianos.com
From this River North location, Maggiano's ode to classic Italian-American neighborhoods has spawned spin-offs around the country. Fans love it for its big-hearted spirit as expressed in huge portions of familiar red-sauced pastas and the genuine warmth of servers and staff. But be forewarned: it's loud and crowded, better suited to convivial groups than to intimacy-seeking couples. Italian menu. Lunch, dinner. Closed Dec 25. Bar. Casual attire. Valet parking. Outdoor seating. **$$**

★★ MAZA (MAP E)
2748 N Lincoln Ave (60657)
Phone 773/929-9600
Chicago's not strong on Middle Eastern eats, but it hardly needs to be with a standout like Maza. This unassuming Lincoln Park spot specializes in small-plate appetizers that could constitute a grazer's meal. When you're ready to commit to something more substantial, try the shawirma or the rack of lamb. Complete your thematic meal with a bottle of Lebanese red wine. Lebanese menu. Dinner. Casual attire. **$$**

★★ MENAGERIE 84 (MAP E)
1232 W Belmont (60657)
Phone 773/404-8333

Across the street from the Theatre Building in Lakeview, Menagerie aims to please audiences with creative modern American meals. The co-chefs—whose résumés include past stints at such high-profile restaurants as Bistro 110, Spring, and Green Dolphin Street—do best when they dare the most. Fish and chips are reinvented here in an Asian style, and duck confit is paired with macaroni and cheese. For-sale works of local artists decorate the walls. Expect a sizable bar crowd for drinks and nibbles post-curtain. Eclectic/International menu. Lunch, dinner. Closed Tues. Bar. Casual attire. Outdoor seating. **$$**

the hot dog

The humble weiner, although German in origin, has been as American as apple pie since its first mention at the turn of the 20th century. From its association with picnics, outdoor fun, and sporting events, the hot dog has ingrained itself in our collective idea of what a perfect, hand-held meal should be. No wonder the National Hot Dog and Sausage Council estimates that more than 155 million hot dogs are consumed over the July 4 weekend alone.

The earliest known mention of the phrase "hot dog" was a story in the Yale Record of 1895, in which students "contentedly munched hot dogs." Even this reference has been heatedly debated as the origins of this most American of imports are called into question. Regardless of where it came from, the hot dog is here to stay as a fixture in cafeterias and on city streets throughout this country.

There are so many variations on the classic hot dog that one could spend days experimenting with ratios of chili to cheese, onions to relish, mustard to ketchup. The options can be overwhelming. In the realm of street food, two main contenders have emerged, each with a loyal following.

New Yorkers like their hot dogs long, skinny, and slathered with tangy sauerkraut. The hot dog itself has to be nicely grilled or broiled to give it a pleasant texture, and a plain bun is preferred. Mustard is acceptable in some areas, but keep the ketchup far away. Caramelized onions complete the picture for the perfect New York hot dog. Fine specimens can be found at Gray's Papaya and Papaya King, but the best examples of a perfect New York hot dog can be procured from the carts of the many street vendors who will make a quick one to order with all the panache New Yorkers are known for.

For a completely different take on hot dogs, you have to go to Chicago, where a perfect hot dog is an art form unto itself. Although New Yorkers can't seem to understand why anyone would want a "salad" on their hot dog, Chicagoans take the expansive ingredient list very seriously and put much care into crafting the perfect hot dog. In this town, poppy seed buns are the name of the game, and the dogs themselves had better be steamed and hot. Hot chili peppers, chunks of tomato, relish, onions, mustard, and, last but not least, a sharp dill pickle spear complete this concoction. Great examples of classic Chicago hot dogs can be found at The Wiener's Circle (2622 N Clark St), Gold Coast Dogs (159 N Wabash Ave), and the local Portillo's chain (635½ W North Ave, Villa Park). All three have multiple locations throughout the city.

About the only thing New York and Chicago hot dogs have in common is a distain for ketchup. This, however, is enough to keep the peace, and we can all thank the humble hot dog for it.

★★ MIA FRANCESCA   (MAP C)
3311 N Clark St (60657)
Phone 773/281-3310
Fax 773/281-6671
www.miafrancesca.com

The original of an ever-expanding family of restaurants, still-trendy (and loud) Mia Francesca packs 'em in for the earthy, ever-changing, moderately priced northern Italian fare. The casually stylish, colorful crowd is comprised of all ages and persuasions; the décor manages to be simultaneously sleek and warm. The second floor is a bit calmer; the outdoor tables are a lucky score for summer dining. Long waits at the vintage bar or in the coach house are often part of the dining experience here, as Mia takes no reservations. Italian menu. Closed Thanksgiving, Dec 25. Dinner. Bar. Children's menu. Valet parking. Outdoor seating. **$$**

★ ★ MIKE DITKA'S **86** (MAP A)
100 E Chestnut St (60611)
Phone 312/587-8989
www.mikeditkaschicago.com

Former Chicago Bears coach Mike Ditka's namesake restaurant is manly, naturally, yet surprisingly civilized. While a museum installation-quality sports memorabilia display decorates the clubby restaurant, the patrons exhibit more steakhouse than stadium behavior. Conveniently located near the Magnificent Mile and its many hotels and shopping destinations, Ditka's dishes up generous portions of quality meats (including a massive signature pork chop and "training table" pot roast), as well as seafood, pastas, and salads. The cigar-friendly bar is a louder, more casual destination for snacks and televised sports; upstairs, the cigar lounge features live piano music. American menu. Lunch, dinner, brunch. Closed Dec 25. Bar. Children's menu. Casual attire. Outdoor seating. **$$$**

★ ★ ★ MK **87** (MAP A)
868 N Franklin St (60610)
Phone 312/482-9179
Fax 312/482-9171
www.mkchicago.com

Style meets substance at Michael Kornick's mk, where refined yet real contemporary cuisine is offered in a perfectly compatible setting. The seasonal American food is clean and uncontrived, the multitiered architectural space linear and neutral without severity. Mergers (stylish couples) and acquisitions (salt-and-pepper-haired types in fashionable eyewear) are all a part of the mk dining experience—as are knowledgeable service, a fine wine list (including private-label selections), and excellent desserts. Degustation menus are available, and the chic lounge area is perfect for a before-or-after glass of bubbly. American menu. Dinner. Closed holidays; also the week of July 4. Bar. **$$$**

★ ★ ★ MON AMI GABI **88** (MAP B)
2300 N Lincoln Park W (60614)
Phone 773/348-8886
www.monamigabi.com

This charming (and aromatic) setting in Lincoln Park's Belden Stratford is so French, you may start speaking with an accent. Solid bistro fare, including a juicy selection of steak preparations and fresh fruits de mer, is a big draw, as are the cozy ambience and rolling wine cart. A second location is in west-suburban Oak Brook, in Oakbrook Center (phone 630/472-1900). French bistro menu. Dinner. Closed holidays. Bar. Children's menu. Casual attire. Outdoor seating. **$$**

★★ MONSOON   (MAP B)

2813 N Broadway (60657)
Phone 773/665-9463

A fascinating menu of contemporary Indian-Asian fusion is presented in an exotic, erotic setting. It's easy to give yourself over to your senses in this upscale opium den dining room; between courses of intriguing food and creative cocktails, you can catch the action in the open kitchen (with tandoor oven) or study the Kama Sutra artwork in the rest rooms. Pan-Asian menu. Dinner. Closed Mon. Bar. Casual attire. Outdoor seating. **$$$**

★★★ MORTON'S OF CHICAGO   **90** (MAP A)

1050 N State St (60610)
Phone 312/266-4820
Fax 312/266-4852
www.mortons.com

This steakhouse chain, which originated in Chicago in 1978, appeals to serious meat lovers. With a selection of belt-busting carnivorous delights (like the house specialty, a 24-ounce porterhouse), as well as fresh fish, lobster, and chicken entrées, Morton's rarely disappoints. If you just aren't sure what you're in the mood for, the tableside menu presentation may help you decide. Here, main course selections are placed on a cart that's rolled to your table, where servers describe each item in detail. Steak menu. Dinner. Closed holidays. Bar. Casual attire. Valet parking. **$$$**

★★★ NACIONAL 27   (MAP A)

325 W Huron (60610)
Phone 312/664-2727
www.leye.com

The name hints at the 27 Latin countries informing the menu at this stylish, even sexy, River North restaurant. Exotic ingredients and creative preparations (including some refreshingly different desserts) lend an escapist feel to a meal here; an array of tapas is one dining option. The ambience is upscale, contemporary supper club, with a posh lounge that's a popular gathering place for after-work or date drinks. Things really heat up on weekends with late-night deejay dancing (with a cover charge for non-diners). Latin American menu. Dinner. Closed Sun. Bar. Casual attire. Outdoor seating. **$$$**

★ ★ ★ NAHA (MAP A)

500 N Clark St (60610)
Phone 312/321-6242
Fax 312/321-7561
www.naha-chicago.com

Chef Carrie Nahabadian cooked at the Four Seasons Beverly Hills before opening her own River North spot, Naha, where she merges her Armenian background with her California training. The result is a luscious Mediterranean-like blend of flavors in creative dishes such as sea scallops with grapefruit, bass with olive oil-poached tomatoes, and roast pheasant with grilled asparagus. The sleek, sophisticated décor and attentive service vault Naha above area competitors. American menu. Lunch, dinner. Closed Sun; holidays. Bar. Casual attire. Outdoor seating. **$$$**

★ ★ NANIWA (MAP A)

607 N Wells St (60610)
Phone 312/255-8555
www.sushinaniwa.com

You don't expect an overlooked gem of a restaurant to be housed on busy Wells Street in River North. But Naniwa is hidden in plain sight. Distinct from the many trendy sushi joints that double as lounges, Naniwa plays it straight with good, fresh fish and deluxe maki rolls. Indoor tables are close together, but in season the patio offers prime viewing of the passing parades of people on Wells. Open for lunch, Naniwa does a big to-go business with area office workers. Japanese menu. Lunch, dinner. Bar. Children's menu. Casual attire. Reservations recommended. Outdoor seating. **$$**

★ ★ NIX 94 (MAP A)

163 E Walton Pl (60611)
Phone 312/867-7575; toll-free 866/866-8086
Fax 312/751-9205
www.millenium-hotels.com

This stylishly modern, eclectic offering in the Millennium Knickerbocker Hotel serves a breakfast buffet, lunch, and dinner, with selections running the gamut from upscale comfort food to global fusion. The crowd is a mix of business types and traveling families. Don't miss the 44-strong martini list. American menu. Breakfast, lunch, dinner, Sun brunch. Bar. Children's menu. Casual attire. Valet parking. Outdoor seating. **$$$**

★ ★ ★ NOMI  (MAP A)
800 N Michigan Ave (60611)
Phone 312/239-4030
Fax 312/239-4029
www.nomirestaurant.com

A posh perch over Chicago's famed Magnificent Mile, NoMI (an acronym for North Michigan) is the Park Hyatt's stylish, civilized destination for critically acclaimed contemporary French cuisine. Asian influences are evident in sushi and sashimi selections on the sophisticated menu. Luxurious materials combine in the streamlined décor, highlighted by an eye-catching art collection, glittering open kitchen, and scintillating view from floor-to-ceiling windows. The wine list is both impressive and extensive, with 3,000 or so bottles. NoMI also serves breakfast and lunch and offers outdoor terrace dining in fair weather. French menu. Breakfast, lunch, dinner. Bar. Reservations recommended. Outdoor seating. **$$$$**

★ ★ ★ NORTH POND (MAP B)
2610 N Cannon Dr (60614)
Phone 773/477-5845
Fax 773/477-3234
www.northpondrestaurant.com

North Pond delivers a dining experience like no other. Seasonal, contemporary American food emphasizing regional ingredients is paired with an all-American wine list and served in a one-of-a-kind location on the Lincoln Park lagoon. The handsome Arts and Crafts décor gives the feeling that Frank Lloyd Wright had a hand in the proceedings. No roads lead here; cab it or look for parking along Cannon Drive, and then follow the garden path to the restaurant. Sunday brunch is a refined indulgence, and outdoor dining is a special treat in seasonable weather. Menu changes seasonally. American menu. Dinner, Sun brunch. Closed Mon; holidays. Outdoor seating. **$$$**

★ OAK TREE (MAP A)
900 N Michigan Ave (60611)
Phone 312/751-1988

With its location on the sixth floor of the busy indoor mall at 900 North Michigan (known to locals as the Bloomingdale's Building), Oak Tree is a popular spot with shoppers and tourists who need a break from the hustle and bustle of the Magnificent Mile. The varied menu features everything from Americanized versions of Asian, Mexican, and Italian dishes to dressed-up breakfast items (served all day) such as pancakes, omelets, and eggs Benedict. If you can't snag a window seat to enjoy the views of Michigan Avenue, don't worry—the bright, nature-inspired dining room makes for a pleasurable experience nonetheless. American menu. Breakfast, lunch, dinner. Closed holidays. Children's menu. Casual attire. **$**

★ ORANGE   (MAP B)
3231 N Clark St (60657)
Phone 773/549-4400

This Wrigleyville breakfast and lunch spot made its mark in the restaurant-mad neighborhood with inventive fare like "green eggs and ham" (pesto eggs and pancetta), jelly donut pancakes, and steak sandwiches with Spanish blue cheese. The juice bar will squeeze anything garden-grown, from oranges to cucumbers and beets. The colorful interior, family-friendly vibe, and budget-minded menu spread good cheer here. American menu. Brunch. Children's menu. Casual attire. Outdoor seating. **$**

★ ★ ★ PANE CALDO   (MAP A)
72 E Walton St (60611)
Phone 312/649-0055
Fax 312/274-0540
www.pane-caldo.com

This little gem off the Magnificent Mile is home to some of the best northern Italian food this side of Piedmont. It's easy to miss this tiny restaurant—look for the ultra-posh shoppers enjoying a midday respite and the suit-coated businessmen having power lunches over risotto Milanese. An extensive wine list complements the kitchen's lovely creations, made with organic meats and locally grown organic produce. Italian menu. Lunch, dinner. Closed Mon. Bar. Business casual attire. Reservations recommended. **$$$**

pizza—a chicago original

Chicagoans have never been satisfied with the ordinary. From the world's largest airport to the world's tallest building (until 1998—now North America's tallest), Chicago does things in a big way. No wonder the city that turned a regular brownstone into the world's first skyscraper also transformed the familiar pizza pie into what we now know as the Chicago-style pizza.

It must be noted that Chicago-style pizza has about as much in common with a normal thin-crust pizza as a bicycle does with a tank. Both have some type of tomato sauce and cheese, but all similarities end there. Contrary to popular belief, the crust on a classic Chicago pizza isn't thick at all. It's actually a normal pizza crust that is put into a special pizza pan with deep sides. This crust is then built up the sides of the pan to form the familiar "deep dish" shape.

The first thing laid onto the crust, however, isn't the sauce; it's the cheese, which is pressed down to make a nice bed for all of the other ingredients. At this point, it's up to the pizza maker to decide what goes in next. Remember, it's bad form for the crust around the edge to perch over the pizza, so this space must be filled with three to four times the quantity of ingredients on a normal pizza. Sausage is a must, and is cited as the most frequently requested ingredient on pizzas in the city. Peppers, onions, pepperoni, olives, and all of the best-loved standbys of the classic pizza are piled high to fill that waiting crust.

After the ingredients are selected and placed, the last item—a thick, chunky tomato sauce—is added. It is poured liberally over the ingredients and then sprinkled with a light dusting of cheese before baking. Good things come to those who wait, and Chicago-style pizza is no exception; average baking times hover around the 45-minute mark at Chicago's most famous pizzerias.

When the pizza finally comes out of the oven, one piece is a meal unto itself. Two will prevent the need for breakfast. And three slices will make you famous in this city of "big shoulders." The original home of Chicago-style pizza can be found at **Pizzeria Uno** (29 E Ohio St; phone 312/321-1000); its sister restaurant, **Pizzeria Due** (619 N Wabash Ave; phone 312/943-2400), is just down the street. **Lou Malnati's** (439 N Wells St; phone 312/828-9800), started by a former Pizzeria Uno chef, is another windy city original, while **Gino's East** (633 N Wells; phone 312/943-1124) rounds out the listings for great Chicago-style pizza. Regardless of where you stop, though, you're sure to find great pizza in Chicago.

★★PAPAGUS GREEK TAVERNA (MAP A)
620 N State St (60610)
Phone 312/642-8450; toll-free 888/538-8823
Fax 312/642-8132
www.leye.com
Chicago hit-making restaurant group Lettuce Entertain You runs Papagus, a crowd-pleaser for rustic Greek tavern-style food. In addi-

tion to Grecian staples like flaming cheese, eggplant spread, and roast lamb, Papagus serves a variety of authentic small plates that encourage experimentation. Pair them affably with a bottle from the list of imported Greek wines. Greek menu. Lunch, dinner. Bar. Children's menu. Casual attire. Valet parking. Outdoor seating. **$$**

★ PENNY'S NOODLE SHOP (MAP C)

3400 N Sheffield Ave (60657)
Phone 773/281-8222

Hungry bargain-hunters have been slurping up Penny's namesake noodles by the carload ever since this convenient (and expanding) concept opened its doors a few years ago. Draws include the healthful fare, low prices, and low-key atmosphere. Thai menu. Lunch, dinner. Closed Mon; holidays. Casual attire. Outdoor seating. **$**

★ ★ ★ PILI PILI 101 (MAP A)

230 W Kinzie St (60610)
Phone 877/878-0553
www.pilipilirestaurant.com

A contemporary take on the earthy fare of Provence and neighboring Mediterranean regions is offered in a tastefully rustic setting. Expect pure flavors that come from fresh seasonal ingredients, with many dishes emanating from the aromatic wood-burning rotisserie or brick oven. The well-chosen, French-focused wine list includes some flights. Grand aioli and charcuterie presentations draw the eye to the center of the dining room; a smaller café area is open all day. The unusual name comes from a North African hot pepper used in a regional infused oil. Mediterranean menu. Lunch, dinner. Bar. Casual attire. Outdoor seating. **$$$**

★ PIZZERIA UNO (MAP A)

29 E Ohio St (60611)
Phone 312/321-1000
www.unos.com

Surely you've heard about Chicago-style pizza: the kind made of a flaky, pie-like crust and stuffed with generous amounts of meats, cheeses, vegetables, and spices. This legendary deep-dish pizza originated at Pizzeria Uno, a casual eatery decorated with hardwood booths and pictures of famous Chicagoans. Because these pizzas take up to 45 minutes to prepare, your order is taken while you wait for your table. Not willing to wait for a seat? Head across the street to Pizzeria Due, which was opened to handle the overflow of crowds at Pizzeria Uno. Pizza. Lunch, dinner. Closed Thanksgiving, Dec 25. Bar. Children's menu. Casual attire. Outdoor seating. **$**

★★ PREGO RISTORANTE (MAP E)
2901 N Ashland Ave (60657)
Phone 773/472-9190

Housed in a modest storefront, Prego is a welcome addition to busy
Ashland Avenue in Lakeview. Candles and paper-topped tables provide warmth, as does a caring owner who frequently patrols the floor
looking after guests. Although the menu changes often to reflect the
season, hits include risotto, squash ravioli, and fish specials (offered
regularly). The fare is no match for downtown challengers, but in the
neighborhood, Prego is a charmer. Italian menu. Lunch, dinner. Closed
Sun-Mon. Bar. Casual attire. Outdoor seating. **$$**

★★★ PUMP ROOM 104 (MAP B)
1301 N State Pkwy (60610)
Phone 312/266-0360
Fax 312/266-1798
www.pumproom.com

This revered Chicago classic combines the grand, gracious hotel din-
ing of yesteryear with contemporary French-American fare. Having
undergone several chef changes in recent years (and a major renova-
tion a few years ago), the Pump Room remains popular with tourists
and special-occasion celebrants. Booth One lives on, complete with
vintage telephone; the bar could have been transported from a *Thin
Man* set. The photo wall is a sentimental journey down the memory
lane of film, music, and politics. Highlights include live music with
a small dance floor and Sunday Champagne brunch. The "upscale
casual" dress code attests to the times. American menu. Breakfast,
lunch, dinner, Sun brunch. Bar. Valet parking. **$$$**

★★ RAS DASHEN 105 (MAP G)
5846 N Broadway (60660)
Phone 773/506-9601
Fax 773/506-9685

Feel free to eat with your hands at Ras Dashen, an Ethiopian eatery
that provides an authentic taste of the North African nation. In native
style, diners tear hunks of the spongy inerja bread that forms a plate for
chicken and lamb dishes and use it to scoop up tasty bites. Ethiopian
art and artifacts, including imported straw tables and chairs, fill the tidy
Uptown storefront. Ethiopian menu. Lunch, dinner. Closed Tues. Bar.
Casual attire. Reservations recommended. **$$**

★ REDFISH (MAP A)

400 N State St (60610)
Phone 312/467-1600
Fax 312/467-0325
www.redfishamerica.com

This thematic Cajun spot goes all out with "N'awlins" décor, a catch-all of voodoo dolls, Mardis Gras masks, and hot sauces. The namesake redfish leads the menu (have it blackened) along with crab-stuffed salmon and pastas. In keeping with its Big Easy affinity, drinking is a sport here. To encourage late-night guzzling, the restaurant brings in zydeco and R & B bands on the weekends. Cajun menu. Lunch, dinner. Closed Easter, Thanksgiving, Dec 25. Bar. Children's menu. Casual attire. Valet parking. Outdoor seating. **$$**

★ ★ RIVA (MAP A)

700 E Grand Ave (60611)
Phone 312/644-7482
Fax 312/206-7035
www.stefanirestaurants.com

Bustling with Navy Pier tourists and locals alike, this elegant restaurant is popular for its fresh seafood, as well as its spectacular views of the Chicago skyline. Along with a 40-foot-long open kitchen, the dining room features nautical décor that re-creates the atmosphere of the Italian Riviera. On Wednesdays (9:30 pm) and Saturdays (10:15 pm) from Memorial Day to Labor Day, enjoy Navy Pier's dazzling evening fireworks displays while you dine. Seafood menu. Lunch, dinner. Closed Thanksgiving, Dec 24-25. Bar. Children's menu. Casual attire. Valet parking. Outdoor seating. **$$**

★ ★ ROY'S 108 (MAP A)

720 N State (60610)
Phone 312/787-7599
roysrestaurant.com

Don't expect luau fare—and don't wear your Hawaiian shirt—at this sleek, contemporary Hawaiian chain member. Lots of creative seafood dishes populate the menu, with several unusual fish varieties offered; French and Asian fusion elements are evident throughout. There are also several meat dishes for the seafood squeamish. Menu selections are listed with suggested wine pairings (the restaurant has its own wine label produced by various houses—plus its own range of sake, which partners nicely with much of the food). Hawaiian menu. Dinner. Bar. Children's menu. Casual attire. Outdoor seating. **$$$**

★ ★ SAI CAFÉ (MAP E)

2010 N Sheffield Ave (60614)
Phone 773/472-8080
www.saicafe.com

This old-guard Lincoln Park neighborhood standby for sushi and classic Japanese cuisine was crowded long before the wave of hip sushi spots hit town. It's a comfortable, low-attitude place for reliable fare and friendly service—and the selection of both sushi and maki rolls is extensive. Sushi menu. Dinner. Bar. Casual attire. Reservations recommended. **$$**

★ ★ THE SALOON (MAP A)

200 E Chestnut St (60611)
Phone 312/280-5454
Fax 312/280-6986
www.saloonsteakhouse.com

If you're looking for a light bite, The Saloon is not the place to go. This classic steakhouse offers mega-sized portions of meat-heavy fare, like the 2-pound porterhouse and the 14-ounce strip loin. Located on a somewhat secluded strip just off of busy Michigan Avenue, The Saloon is the perfect place for escaping the crowds of power shoppers on the Magnificent Mile. Steak menu. Lunch, dinner. Closed holidays. Bar. Casual attire. **$$$**

★ ★ ★ SALPICON 111 (MAP B)

1252 N Wells St (60610)
Phone 312/988-7811
Fax 312/988-7715
www.salpicon.com

In a town where chef Rick Bayless and his Frontera Grill (see) rule the gourmet Mexican roost, Salpicon remains an in-the-know treasure. Chef Priscilla Satkoff grew up in Mexico City and honors her native cuisine here with rich moles, tender roasted meats, and upscale twists on both, such as ancho chile quail. The extensive wine list, managed by the chef's husband, has won numerous awards. But it's hard to get past the 50-some tequilas on offer to mix in margaritas (knowing servers ably steer agave gringos). Salpicon's boldly colored interiors generate a spirit of fiesta. Mexican menu. Dinner, Sun brunch. Closed Thanksgiving, Dec 25. Bar. Valet parking. Outdoor seating. **$$**

★ SAUCE 112 (MAP B)

1750 N Clark St (60614)
Phone 312/932-1750
Fax 312/932-0056
www.saucechicago.com

Opposite Lincoln Park on the fringe of Old Town, Sauce intends to be a restaurant. But a pack of young, martini-swilling regulars have claimed it as a hangout. The menu ranges far and wide to include bar fare (artichoke dip, quesadillas, pizza), comfort food (lasagna), and trendy options (seared tuna). If you're only after the food, come early. But if it's eye candy you crave, drop by late. American menu. Lunch, dinner, late-night. Closed Sun; Jan 1, Dec 25. Bar. Casual attire. Outdoor seating. **$$**

★ SAYAT NOVA 113 (MAP A)

157 E Ohio St (60611)
Phone 312/644-9159
Fax 312/644-6234

For something completely different, try this family-run Armenian spot for a touch of foreign intrigue and bargain-priced kebabs, lamb dishes, stuffed grape leaves, and other traditional Middle Eastern fare. Opened in 1969, Sayat Nova is now a pleasant anachronism in its chichi off-Mag Mile location. Middle Eastern menu. Lunch, dinner. Closed holidays. Bar. **$$**

★★ SCOOZI 114 (MAP D)

410 W Huron (60610)
Phone 312/943-5900
Fax 312/943-8969
www.leye.com

An early pioneer of now-booming River North, this Lettuce Entertain You Italian concept—once hip, now comfortable—is a convivial place to gather for cocktails in the large bar area, cracker-crust pizzas, goodies from the generous antipasto bar, or full-blown Italian dining. The cavernous space gets warmth and gravitas from the faux-antiqued décor. Italian menu. Lunch, dinner. Closed Thanksgiving, Dec 25. Bar. Valet parking. Outdoor seating. **$$**

★★★★ SEASONS 115 (MAP A)

120 E Delaware Pl (60611)
Phone 312/649-2349
Fax 312/649-2372
www.fourseasons.com/chicagofs

Dining at Seasons, the upscale and elegant restaurant of the Four Seasons Hotel Chicago, is the sort of experience that may cause whiplash. Your head will whip back and forth as you watch stunning plates pass by in the rich and refined dining room. Each dish looks better than the next. On a nightly basis, the dining room is filled with food envy. Perhaps this is because the kitchen prepares every plate with a deep respect for ingredients, making every inventive dish on the menu of New American fare a delight to admire from afar and devour from up close. The chef offers five-course and eight-course tasting menus. What's more, while a restaurant of this stature could easily feel pretentious, the staff's warmth and charm makes dining here easy and comfortable—a pleasure from start to finish. American, French menu. Lunch, dinner, Sun brunch. Bar. Piano, jazz trio Sat. Children's menu. Valet parking. Casual attire. **$$$$**

★ ★ ★ SHANGHAI TERRACE (MAP A)
108 E Superior (60610)
Phone 312/573-6744
chicago.peninsula.com
Fittingly, the Asian-run Peninsula Hotel gives Chicago its best Chinese restaurant. Intimate, and trimmed in rich hues of ruby red and lacquer black, Shanghai Terrace is the best looking of its category too. Start with the eatery's refined three-bite dim sum dishes. Save room for flavorful entrées like spicy Sichuan beef and wok-fried lobster. You'll find Shanghai Terrace one level below the ornate hotel lobby. The restaurant adjoins an expansive terrace offering al fresco dining in the summer six stories above Michigan Avenue. Chinese menu. Lunch, dinner. Closed Sun-Mon. Bar. Casual attire. Outdoor seating. **$$$**

★ ★ SHAW'S CRAB HOUSE (MAP A)
21 E Hubbard St (60611)
Phone 312/527-2722
Fax 312/527-4740
www.shaws-chicago.com
A longtime seafood standard bearer, popular Shaw's in River North goes the extra mile to fly in an extensive variety of fresh seafood, served in a choice of environments—upscale clubby dining room or East Coast-style oyster bar ambience in the Blue Crab Lounge. Seafood menu. Lunch, dinner. Closed Thanksgiving, Dec 25. Bar. Casual attire. Valet parking. Outdoor seating. **$$$**

★★ SHE SHE ⓷⓵⓼ (MAP F)
4539 N Lincoln Ave (60625)
Phone 773/293-3690

Fine dining-caliber food in funky digs endears She She to residents of the Lincoln Square neighborhood. Although the menu changes seasonally, expect chef Nicole Parthemore's signature coconut-crusted shrimp, salmon maki rolls, and contemporized entrées like duck confit linguine. While the food is serious, the scene—from the leopard print seats to the RuPaul martini—is anything but. American menu. Dinner. Closed Mon; Thanksgiving, Dec 25. Bar. Children's menu. Casual attire. Outdoor seating. **$$**

★★ SIGNATURE ROOM AT THE 95TH ⓷⓵⓽ (MAP A)
875 N Michigan Ave (60611)
Phone 312/787-9596
Fax 630/968-7779
www.signatureroom.com

Situated atop one of the world's tallest buildings, the John Hancock, and towering 1,000 feet above the Magnificent Mile, the Signature Room is deservedly famous for its breathtaking vistas. It affords spectacular views from every part of its dining room. Sumptuous Art Deco surroundings complement picture-perfect scenes of the city and Lake Michigan, visible through the floor-to-ceiling windows that circle the room. The food is contemporary American (consider the reasonably priced lunch buffet or the Sunday brunch). Convenient to downtown hotels and shopping, the Signature Lounge is also a popular spot for a romantic rendezvous or business cocktails. American menu. Lunch, dinner, Sun brunch. Closed Jan 1, Dec 25. Bar. Piano. Casual attire. **$$$**

★★★ SPIAGGIA ⓷⓶⓪ (MAP A)
980 N Michigan Ave (60611)
Phone 312/280-2750
Fax 312/943-8560
www.spiaggiarestaurant.com

Next to Spiaggia, you'd have to fly to Milan to get a dose of the sort of contemporary, sophisticated Italian cuisine served here. Chef Tony Mantuano has a light, refined touch, working with artisanal and exotic ingredients like Piemontese beef and seasonal white truffles. Expect frequent menu changes, but typical dishes include wood-roasted scallops with porcini mushrooms and parmesan shavings, pumpkin risotto with seared foie gras, and lamb chops with slow-cooked lamb shoulder. Favored by both expense accounts and special occasion affairs, the opulent trilevel room completes the seduction, offering each table a view over Lake Michigan. Italian menu. Dinner. Closed holidays. Bar. Piano. Jacket required (dinner). Reservations recommended. Valet parking. **$$$$**

★ STANLEY'S (MAP B)
1970 N Lincoln Ave (60614)
Phone 312/642-0007
As you enter through the front door, Stanley's looks like a typical Lincoln Park bar. But walk a little farther into the dining area and you'll feel like you've entered someone's home; this family-friendly space is decorated with photos, children's drawings, and knickknacks. And the food will make you feel at home, too. Large portions of American comfort food like mac and cheese, meatloaf, and mashed potatoes and gravy are sure to bring back memories of the way Mom used to cook. American menu. Lunch, dinner. Bar. Casual attire. Outdoor seating. **$$**

★ SU CASA (122) (MAP A)
49 E Ontario St (60611)
Phone 312/943-4041
Fax 312/943-6480
A River North staple for Tex-Mex, Su Casa has been dishing its brand of south-of-the-border hospitality since 1963. Founded by the same golden-touch restaurateur who established Pizzeria Uno (see), Su Casa sticks to crowd-pleasing favorites like fajitas, chimichangas, and burritos. Colorful Mexican piñatas and murals help generate a fiesta feel. Mexican menu. Lunch, dinner. Closed Thanksgiving, Dec 25. Bar. Valet parking. Outdoor seating. **$$**

★★ SUSHI SAMBA RIO (123) (MAP A)
504 N Wells St (60610)
Phone 312/595-2300
www.sushisamba.com
Flashy and splashy, this New York/Miami import serves up a wild fusion menu of sushi with Japanese and Brazilian dishes—and cocktails to match. The high-concept contemporary décor offers multiple environments (including a crowded bar area), plenty of people-watching, and a nightclub-like ambience when busy. The all-weather rooftop dining area is exposed in summer, enclosed in winter. Japanese, Brazilian menu. Lunch, dinner. Bar. Casual attire. Reservations recommended. Outdoor seating. **$$$**

★ ★ SWK 124 (MAP A)

710 N Wells St (60610)
Phone 312/274-9500
Fax 312/274-0711
www.swankchicago.com

The former nightclub-with-food Swank has morphed into SWK, a restaurant with nightclub sensibilities, meaning that patrons can still enjoy the lounge vibe while indulging in playfully exotic fare like ostrich satay, corn-fried oysters, and "duck, duck, goose" duck breast, foie gras, and goose ravioli. You can dine late in the loftlike spot, but after 11 pm, the music gets louder and the tables are moved back as SWK becomes a swanky lounge anew. American menu. Dinner, late-night. Closed Sun-Mon. Bar. Casual attire. Outdoor seating. **$$$**

★ ★ SZECHWAN EAST 125 (MAP A)

340 E Ohio St (60611)
Phone 312/255-9200
Fax 312/642-3907
www.szechwaneast.com

The refined atmosphere at Szechwan East makes it a fitting resident of the tony Streeterville area. The Chinese restaurant rounds up an appreciative lunch crowd of office workers eager to sample its value-priced lunch buffet. Off-the-menu favorites include hot and sour soup and sesame chicken. Szechwan fare tends to be spicy, but the kitchen will tone it down upon request. Dine after 9 pm on weekends to catch live pop music acts along with your meal. Chinese menu. Dinner, Sun brunch. Closed Thanksgiving. Bar. Valet parking. Outdoor seating. **$$**

★ ★ TIZI MELLOUL 126 (MAP A)

531 N Wells St (60610)
Phone 312/670-4338
Fax 312/670-4254
www.tizimelloul.com

A hipster version of Morocco is as close as a cab ride to River North's Tizi Melloul. Filtered through a modern design sensibility, Tizi references North Africa in its spice market color palette and circular communal dining room lit by lanterns. Grilled octopus, tabbouleh salad, and coriander-roasted duck complete the culinary tour. Come on a Sunday for cocktail-hour belly dancing. Mediterranean menu. Dinner. Closed holidays. Bar. Children's menu. Casual attire. Outdoor seating. **$$**

★★ TOPO GIGIO RISTORANTE (MAP B)
1516 N Wells St (60610)
Phone 312/266-9355

Old Town favorite Topo Gigio draws diners from near and far for crowd-pleasing Italian dishes in a bustling café setting featuring exposed-brick walls and paper-topped tables. The friendly owner also does the cooking and draws up a slate of daily specials to supplement his menu of salads, pastas, and meats. Table waits can be lengthy. For best results, come in summer—early—and snag a table on the outdoor patio or have a drink at the outdoor bar. Italian menu. Lunch, dinner. Bar. Casual attire. Outdoor seating. **$$**

★★★ TOPOLOBAMPO 128 (MAP A)
445 N Clark St (60610)
Phone 312/661-1434
Fax 312/661-1830
www.fronterakitchens.com

Pioneering chef/owner Rick Bayless is a cookbook author, television personality, and perennial culinary award winner with a devoted following. His celebration of the regional cuisines of Mexico is realized at Topolobampo, the upscale counterpart to his famed Frontera Grill (see)—and the shrine where the faithful gather to revel in the bright, earthy flavors of his fine-dining Mexican fare. The seasonal menu is paired with a tome of premium tequilas and an excellent wine list. White tablecloths and colorful folk art help set the tone for a memorable Mexican meal. Mexican menu. Lunch, dinner. Closed Sun-Mon; holidays. Bar. Children's menu. Casual attire. Valet parking. Outdoor seating. **$$$**

★★★★ TRU 129 (MAP A)
676 N Saint Clair St (60611)
Phone 312/202-0001
Fax 312/202-0003
www.trurestaurant.com

Awash in white and set in a chic lofty space, TRU's modern, airy dining room is a stunning stage for chef and co-owner Rick Tramonto's savory, progressive French creations and co-owner pastry chef Gale Gand's incredible, one-of-a-kind sweet and savory endings. Tramonto offers plates filled with flawless ingredients that are treated to his unmatched creativity and artistic flair. The result is food that is precious and, some say, overdone. Indeed, many of the plates are so beautiful and complicated that you may not want to dig in and ruin the presentation, or you may be unable to decipher the appropriate way to consume the dish. TRU offers three- to eight-course "Collections" (prix fixe menus) and a unique and extraordinary four-course dessert and Champagne dessert tasting. Like the savory side of the menu, the desserts have a distinctive sense of ingredient choice, style, and humor. *Secret Inspector's Notes: The details at TRU are adorable, from the small velvet ottomans provided for ladies' purses to the replacement of napkins any time a guest visits the rest room. The service can be inconsistent, and occasionally dishes do not entirely satisfy, but Gale Gand's award-winning desserts and the serenely serious dining environment can make up for any shortcomings.* French menu. Dinner. Closed Sun. Bar. Jacket required. Reservations recommended. Valet parking. **$$$$**

★ TUCCI BENUCCH (MAP A)
900 N Michigan Ave (60611)
Phone 312/266-2500
Fax 312/266-7702
www.leye.com

This is a spot for weary shoppers in the 900 North Michigan Avenue mall to come and relax after they've spent more money than they should have. Tucci Benucch offers reasonably priced (and generously sized) salads, pizzas, and Italian dishes, along with a homey atmosphere. The dining area is modeled after rooms in an Italian country house, with different sections decorated as a sunroom, patio, living room, and barn. Italian menu. Lunch, dinner. Closed Thanksgiving, Dec 25. Bar. Children's menu. Casual attire. **$$**

★ TWIN ANCHORS RESTAURANT AND TAVERN (MAP A)
1655 N Sedgwick St (60614)
Phone 312/266-1616
www.twinanchorsribs.com

Make no bones about it: Chicago is a meat-and-potatoes kind of town, and there are few things that native Chicagoans like more than a great slab of ribs. Choices abound, but a local favorite is Twin Anchors Restaurant and Tavern in the Old Town neighborhood just north of downtown (and a fairly short cab ride away). Although this former speakeasy was reincarnated as a restaurant in 1932, it maintains its hole-in-the-wall appeal, complete with diner-style booths, linoleum tabletops, a jukebox stocked with an eclectic mix of tunes, and an extensive collection of beers. The real attraction, however, is the ribs; rumor has it that they were Frank Sinatra's favorites. Order them zesty, like a local, and then let the feast begin. The menu may be limited, but the portions are generous. If ribs aren't your style, the hamburgers and filet mignon are also excellent. Be prepared for a long wait, though; this 60-seat restaurant fills up fast. Barbecue menu. Lunch, dinner. Bar. Casual attire. **$$**

chicago cooking-related shops

Although eating out is a wildly popular pastime in Chicago, its residents do eat in from time to time. The city's many home stores keep kitchens fully equipped. Here are a few worth checking out:

• **Bloomingdale's Home + Furniture Store.** *600 N Wabash Ave (60611). Phone 312/354-7500.* Set in the historic Medinah Temple, the former home of Chicago's Shriners, this four-level wonder is filled with both architectural and commercial treasures. If the store's ample selection of high-end kitchenware, linens, and home furnishings doesn't grab your attention, the magnificently restored stained-glass windows, soaring dome, and shining facade are sure to have you oohing and ahhing.

• **Crate & Barrel.** *646 N Michigan Ave (60611). Phone 312/787-5900. www.crateandbarrel.com.* This housewares and home furnishings chain got its start in Chicago in 1962 and has since grown to more than 100 stores nationwide. Its large flagship store on Michigan Avenue brings in hordes of visitors drawn in by its clean designs, eye-catching colors, and reasonable prices. The offshoot CB2, at 3757 N Lincoln Ave, targets a younger, urban-chic crowd. Bargain-hunters will love the Crate & Barrel outlet stores at 1864 N Clybourn St, below Trader Joe's, and in west-suburban Naperville at 1860 W Jefferson Ave.

• **Sur La Table.** *50-54 E Walton St (60611). Phone 312/337-0600. www.surlatable.com.* In the 1970s, Seattle spawned this clearinghouse for hard-to-find kitchen gear, and it soon became known as a source for cookware, small appliances, cutlery, kitchen tools, linens, tableware, gadgets, and specialty foods. Sur La Table has since expanded to include cooking classes, chef demonstrations, and cookbook author signings, as well as a catalog and online presence. Cooking connoisseurs discover such finds as cool oven mitts, zest graters, copper whisks, onion soup bowls, and inspired TV dinner trays.

★★ VONG'S THAI KITCHEN   **132** (MAP A)
6 W Hubbard (60610)
Phone 312/644-8664
www.leye.com

This toned-down version of renowned chef Jean-Georges Vongerichten's original, pricier Vong remains a stylish destination for well-crafted Thai-French fusion cuisine. The posh ambience is a bit more casual now, with hip background music, but retains a refined air thanks to rich appointments and polished service. Exotic cocktails enhance the escapist mood; booths in the lounge are a plush place to stop for a sip and a snack. Thai menu. Lunch, dinner. Bar. Children's menu (lunch). Casual attire. Outdoor seating. **$$**

★★ WAVE **133** (MAP A)
644 N Lake Shore Dr (60611)
Phone 312/255-4460
www.whotels.com

Located in the W hotel across from Lake Michigan, Wave delivers ultra-stylish dining in a chic, modern space. The creative, contemporary seafood menu is laced with exotic spices; "tasting plates" are great for grazing with drinks. The loungy bar also offers elaborate cold seafood concoctions from the "ice bar" paired with high-concept cocktails. Mediterranean menu. Breakfast, lunch, dinner. Bar. Casual attire. Outdoor seating. **$$**

★★ XIPPO **134** (MAP F)
3759 N Damen (60618)
Phone 773/529-9135
www.xippo.com

Velvet chairs, swagged curtains, exposed-brick walls, and a DJ booth transformed a former North Center corner bar into the lounge eatery Xippo. The menu outclasses the average neighborhood saloon in Chicago, with ambitious dishes like pretzel-crusted pork chops and pan-seared duck breast. On weekends, don't be surprised if the young crowd is more likely to have a cake shot than a slice of cake for dessert. American menu. Dinner. Bar. Casual attire. **$$**

★ ★ ★ YOSHI'S CAFÉ ⑬⑤ (MAP C)
3257 N Halsted St (60657)
Phone 773/248-6160
Namesake chef Yoshi Katsumura comes from a fine-dining background, which accounts for the quality and sophistication of his
French-Japanese fusion cuisine. But the longstanding Lakeview café
stays dear to its neighbors by keeping the atmosphere relaxed, fur-
nishing the kind of casual shop that invites repeat dining with good
service and even a children's menu. Although the menu changes
frequently, it maintains the chef's high standards as it meanders
from shrimp cappuccino soup all the way to sirloin steak. Eclectic/
International menu. Lunch, dinner. Closed Mon. Bar. Casual attire.
Outdoor seating. **$$**

★ ★ ★ ZEALOUS ⑬⑥ (MAP D)
419 W Superior St (60610)
Phone 312/475-9112
Fax 312/475-0165
www.zealousrestaurant.com
Charlie Trotter protégé Michael Taus runs Zealous with a Trotter-like
attention to detail and innovation. Menus change constantly, but
you can expect the daring, like veal sweetbread-topped beignets, taro
root and mushroom ravioli with sea-urchin sauce, and star-anise
braised veal cheeks. Put yourself in the chef's hands with a five- or
seven-course degustation menu. This is event dining, amplified by the
thoughtful Asian-influenced décor. Bamboo planters, skylit 18-foot
ceilings, and a glass-clad wine room make Zealous a fitting resident
of the River North gallery district. American menu. Lunch, dinner.
Closed Sun-Mon; holidays. Bar. Casual attire. Reservations recom-
mended. **$$$**

West Side

Many of the neighborhoods on Chicago's west side have experienced frequent shifts in ethnicity. In Wicker Park, for example, working-class Polish gave way to working-class Latino, which in recent years have given way to an influx of style-conscious artists, hipsters, and white-collar professionals. The latter shift has resulted in the opening of many trendy restaurants, bars, and shops. A similar gentrification has taken place in nearby Bucktown.

The Ukrainian Village (west of Damen Avenue and north of Chicago Avenue) has also become more gentrified. Nonetheless, "Ukie Village," as it's commonly called, retains its old-world charm and grace. Stop by the Sts. Volodymyr and Olha Ukrainian Catholic Church, situated at Chicago Avenue and Oakley Boulevard, and you'll feel as though you've been transported to a different time and place. Hold on to that feeling by checking out the Ukrainian National Museum, a celebration of all things Ukrainian.

Just to the east of Ukranian Village, on North Milwaukee Avenue, you can visit the Polish Museum of America. Founded in 1935, the museum houses 60,000 volumes of work covering Polish history and culture.

Farther south, the Mexican Fine Arts Center Museum features the works of new and established Mexican artists. The museum is located in the Pilsen/Little Village community, considered the cultural heart of Chicago's Mexican population.

Sports fans will want to pay a visit to the United Center on West Madison Avenue, especially if one of its two occupants—the NBA's Bulls and the NHL's Blackhawks—has a home game. Outside the arena, a bronze statue of Michael Jordan celebrates his achievements. "His Airness" guided the Bulls to six world championships during the 1990s.

For those seeking serenity, the Garfield Park Conservatory features a wide variety of floral and plant life within its six massive greenhouses. Located on Central Park Avenue, the conservatory is open every day of the year. Better yet, admission and parking are free.

Chicago has always been known for its ethnic diversity, and perhaps no area of Chicago better represents this diversity than the city's west side. Hundreds of thousands of first-generation Americans called the west side home in the late 1800s and early 1900s. They emigrated from nations such as Italy, Poland, Russia, and Greece in search of a better life, but many faced impoverished conditions when they settled in the densely populated area. Conditions improved when social reformer Jane Addams founded Hull-House in 1889 on the city's near west side. Hull-House provided such services as day care for the children of working mothers, help in finding employment, and English and citizenship classes. Addams continued her social work well into the 1900s. For her efforts, she was awarded the Nobel Peace Prize in 1931. Today, you can learn more about her work and the city's near west side by visiting the Jane Addams Hull-House Museum at 800 South Halsted.

Restaurants on the West Side

★ AMARIND'S 137 (MAP G)
6822 W North Ave (60607)
Phone 773/889-9999
Amarind's creative and inexpensive fare may well warrant a drive out to the western edge of the city (Amarind's is closer to suburban River Forest than to downtown). The chef/owner hails from Arun's (see), the north side gourmet eatery consistently ranked as one of the country's best Thai restaurants. His experience shows in offerings such as spicy curry pork, ginger scallop salad, and spinach noodles with shrimp and crab. With the exception of a couple of "market price" items, nothing tops $11 here. Thai menu. Lunch, dinner. Closed Mon. Casual attire. Reservations recommended. **$$**

★ ★ ★ ARUN'S 138 (MAP G)
4156 N Kedzie Ave (60618)
Phone 773/539-1909
Fax 773/539-2125
www.arunsthai.com
Arun's version of Thai food is as similar to neighborhood take-out as caviar is to peanut butter. Regarded as the best Thai interpreter in the city, if not the country, Arun's takes a fine-dining turn with the complex cooking of Thailand, but without the attendant snobbery of many serious restaurants. A phalanx of eager, well-informed servers cheerfully work the alcove-lodged tables in the tranquil, Asian-art-filled rooms. Chef Arun Sampanthavivat prepares an original prix fixe menu nightly, proffering 12 courses, half of them small appetizers, served family style. You won't know what's on until you arrive, but the kitchen easily adapts to food and spice sensitivities. Thai menu. Dinner. Closed Mon; holidays. Bar. Reservations recommended. **$$$$**

★ ★ AVEC (MAP D)

615 W Randolph St (60661)
Phone 312/377-2002

Thinking man's Mediterranean comfort food is served in a chic sliver of space next to parent restaurant Blackbird (see). An ultra-hip power crowd mingles with restaurant industry insiders; the wood walls, floor, and long communal seating area blend together to create the illusion of an upscale mess hall-cum-sauna. The wine bar concept is fulfilled by a daring list of lesser-known and small-production bottles (40 by the mini-carafe). Mediterranean menu. Dinner, late-night. Bar. Casual attire. Outdoor seating. **$$**

★ ★ AZURÉ (MAP D)

832 W Randolph St (60607)
Phone 312/455-1400

Azuré brings Cal-Ital to Randolph Street's sophisticated restaurant row. Foods native to California, including fish, shellfish, and plenty of fresh produce, get the Italian treatment here. Sample dishes include grilled calamari, the Italian seafood stew cioppino, and chicken Pisa, a dish piled playfully high to resemble the landmark Leaning Tower. Seating options cover two floors. For great views of the city skyline from this West Loop corner locale, opt for a table on the second floor. Italian menu. Dinner. Closed Sun. Bar. Casual attire. Reservations recommended. Outdoor seating. **$$**

★ ★ ★ BLACKBIRD (MAP D)

619 W Randolph St (60606)
Phone 312/715-0708
Fax 312/715-0774
www.blackbirdrestaurant.com

The minimalist chic Blackbird girds style with substance. Aluminum chairs and pale mohair banquettes seat guests at tables within easy eavesdropping distance of one another. But instead of the boring details of someone's career, what you're likely to hear are raves for chef Paul Kahan's French-influenced cooking. Like the décor, his style is spare, hitting just the right contemporary notes without drowning in too many flavors. The market-driven menu changes frequently, with seasonal favorites such as homemade charcuterie, quail with foie gras, and braised veal cheeks. Noise levels are high but the elegantly attired fans who flock here consider it simply good buzz. American menu. Lunch, dinner. Closed Sun; Jan 1, Thanksgiving, Dec 25. Bar. Casual attire. Valet parking. Outdoor seating. **$$$**

★★ BLUE FIN 142 (MAP E)

1952 W North Ave (60622)
Phone 773/394-7373

A good choice for sushi in the Wicker Park/Bucktown area, Blue Fin manages to engender romance in a neighborhood that parties hardy. But its modern sensibility—lots of candlelight and low-key techno music—make it at home in the 'hood. In addition to a good range of raw-based sushi, sashimi, and maki rolls, Blue Fin entertains fans of cooked food with tempura and fish choices on the nicely priced menu. Expect crowds on weekends. Japanese, sushi menu. Dinner. Closed Sun. Casual attire. Outdoor seating. **$$**

★★ BLUEPOINT OYSTER BAR 143 (MAP D)

741 W Randolph St (60661)
Phone 312/207-1222
www.rdgchicago.com

A clubby setting for seafood in the Randolph Market District, upscale Bluepoint is known for its extensive selection of fresh fish and shellfish. The wine list includes a generous array of wines by the glass and the half-bottle. Budget-minded diners might want to consider a lunchtime visit. Seafood menu. Lunch, dinner. Closed holidays. Bar. Children's menu. Casual attire. Outdoor seating. **$$**

★★★ BOB SAN 144 (MAP E)

1805-07 W Division (60622)
Phone 773/235-8888
www.bob-san.com

Sushi-savvy urban diners will appreciate this comfortably hip Wicker Park Japanese entry with a long list of fresh fish offerings that includes a multitude of maki—and entrées are no afterthought. A sequel to Naniwa (see), Bob San maintains the pace with a contemporary, loft-like space, centralized sushi bar, fashionable servers, and a generous sake selection (plus specialty martinis). Sushi chefs will go off the menu for you if they're not too busy. Japanese, sushi menu. Dinner. Bar. Casual attire. Outdoor seating. **$$$**

★★ BONGO ROOM 145 (MAP E)

1470 N Milwaukee Ave (60622)
Phone 773/489-0690

Sleepyheads, mother-daughter duos, and Wicker Park locals of all ages crowd into this funky favorite for bohemian breakfast, Bongo style. Known for long weekend waits, decadent pancakes, and other inventive, seasonal brunch-lunch fare, this is an eclectically decorated, come-as-you-are destination for daytime dining only (no dinner service). American menu. Breakfast, lunch. Bar. Casual attire. **$$**

chicago's outdoor markets

The Windy City's bitterly cold winter weather doesn't lend itself particularly well to outdoor markets, but when the weather warms up in the spring, Chicagoans flock outdoors in search of fresh produce.

Between mid-May and November, you can purchase the best Midwestern fresh fruits, vegetables, and other products at 30 markets throughout the city at the citywide **Farmers Market,** held Tuesday through Thursday and Saturday and Sunday. Hours vary by location; it's usually open 7 am-2 pm unless otherwise noted. *Phone 312/744-3315 (Mayor's Office of Special Events). www.ci.chi.il.us/specialevents.*

Soak up the colorful atmosphere at the city's oldest outdoor market, the **New Maxwell Street Market,** in its new location near downtown. Hone your bargaining skills on everything from food and clothing to antiques and imported goods sold by more than 480 local and international vendors year-round. *Canal St and Roosevelt Rd.*

★★ CAFE ABSINTHE (MAP E)
1954 W North Ave (60622)
Phone 773/278-4488
Fax 773/278-5291
You'd never know what lies behind the walls of this Wicker Park restaurant from the looks of the unassuming façade (and the entrance off an alley behind the building): an intimate and elegant bistro with some of most innovative cuisine in the city. Take note, however, that it is definitely an "urban" experience—the restaurant can become crowded and, at times, very noisy. American menu. Dinner. Closed holidays. **$$$**

★★★ CHEZ JOEL (MAP A)
1119 W Taylor St (60607)
Phone 312/226-6479
Fax 312/226-6589
Just a few minutes from the Loop, tiny Chez Joel dares to be French within the friendly confines of Little Italy. Classic bistro fare (paté, escargots, coquilles St. Jacques, coq au vin, steak frites) is seasoned with more adventurous specials and an appealing sandwich selection at lunch. The cozy room invites with a buttery glow, courtesy of soft yellow walls accented with French prints and posters; in warm weather, the outdoor

garden is a charming oasis. The wine list is moderately priced, and a limited reserve list is offered. Make reservations; the secret is out. French bistro menu. Lunch, dinner. Bar. Casual attire. Outdoor seating. **$$$**

★ ★ CLUB LUCKY (MAP E)

1824 W Wabansia Ave (60622)
Phone 773/227-2300
Fax 773/227-2236
www.clubluckychicago.com

In the 1920s, it was a hardware store. In the 1930s, it was a banquet hall. Throughout the 1980s, it was a bar. Today, the building tucked away on the corner of Honore and Wabansia (smack-dab in the middle of one of the city's hottest neighborhoods, Wicker Park/Bucktown) is Club Lucky, a 1940s-style restaurant and lounge. It's a place to bring a group of friends and enjoy heaping portions of traditional Italian favorites, as well as a martini or two. Italian menu. Dinner. Closed holidays. Children's menu. **$$**

★ COMO 149 (MAP D)

695 N Milwaukee Ave (60622)
Phone 312/733-7400

Longtime Chicago restaurateurs the Marchetti brothers cashed in on the beloved and enormous Como Inn in River West to make room for residential development. They resurfaced with the downscaled Como nearby, trading in their Italian murals and rambling rooms for a contemporary space with soaring headroom. The menu sticks to Italian classics in chicken Vesuvio and pasta Bolognese, the very thing that keeps old Como Inn fans coming around to Como. Italian menu. Dinner. Closed Mon. Bar. Casual attire. Outdoor seating. **$$**

★ ★ FLO 150 (MAP D)

1434 W Chicago Ave (60622)
Phone 312/243-0477

A storefront hidden away on a strip of Chicago Avenue teeming with secondhand shops and dollar stores, Flo is a diamond in the rough. A friendly staff serves fresh and flavorful dishes from the mostly Southwestern-inspired menu in two bright and cozy dining rooms, which are decorated with vibrant pieces of art. Weekend brunch packs in crowds who wait in line for hearty egg dishes like huevos rancheros and chilaquiles, as well as for the blueberry and strawberry pancakes with homemade syrup. Mexican menu. Breakfast, lunch, dinner, brunch. Closed Mon. Casual attire. Reservations recommended. **$$**

★★ GLORY (MAP E)
1952 N Damen Ave (60647)
Phone 773/235-7400
Occupying a classically sunken Bucktown bungalow, Glory looks very Chicago, but its menu has a strong New England accent. It dares to go East Coastal with seafood, carving a unique niche for itself on the competitive culinary scene. Start with Ipswich clams and Johnny cakes, but save room for the lobster pot pie and substantial clam bake, which includes shrimp, lobster, and sausage as well as clams. Casual digs and affordable pricing make this neighborhood gem worthy of repeat visits. American, seafood menu. Breakfast, lunch, dinner. Bar. Children's menu. Casual attire. Outdoor seating. **$$**

★★ IXCAPUZALCO 152 (MAP G)
2919 N Milwaukee Ave (60618)
Phone 773/486-7340
Fax 773/486-7348
Authentic, regional Mexican fare is the draw at this unpretentious neighborhood storefront. While a few dishes are recognizable renditions, Ixcapuzalco presents an opportunity to savor more intriguing, less familiar preparations for lunch, dinner, or Sunday brunch. There's also a traditional mole of the day, paired with a variety of meats. Dozens of premium tequilas may be sipped or shaken into margaritas. Candlelight and white tablecloths, rustic hand-carved wood chairs, and brilliant-hued artwork warm the small, smoke-free main dining room (which can be noisy due to the presence of the small, open kitchen; the back room is quieter). Mexican menu. Lunch, dinner, Sun brunch. Closed Tues. Bar. Casual attire. **$$$**

★★ JANE'S 153 (MAP E)
1655 W Cortland St (60622)
Phone 773/862-5263
www.janesresaurant.com
Befitting the Bucktown location, this eclectic American girl is something of a funky flower child. The quaint setting and creative menu offerings (including some vegetarian choices) make it a favorite of neighborhood denizens and dating couples. American menu. Dinner, brunch. Closed holidays. Bar. Casual attire. Outdoor seating. **$$**

★ ★ ★ LA SARDINE (MAP D)
111 N Carpenter St (60607)
Phone 312/421-2800
Fax 312/421-2318
www.lasardine.com

Perhaps a bit large for a bistro, La Sardine nevertheless delivers the requisite aromas, creature comforts, and menu classics. Warm and bustling (and sometimes noisy) despite a fairly industrial location, La Sardine draws both hip and mature urbanites for the likes of escargots, brandade, bouillabaisse, roast chicken, and profiteroles. Servers wear butcher aprons; the walls are buttery yellow; and those scents waft from an open kitchen and rotisserie. The impressive wine list includes some hard-to-find French selections. French menu. Lunch, dinner. Closed Sun; holidays. Bar. Casual attire. **$$**

★ ★ LE BOUCHON (MAP E)
1958 N Damen Ave (60647)
Phone 773/862-6600
Fax 773/524-1208
www.lebouchonofchicago.com

Tiny Le Bouchon is known almost as much for its cozy, oh-so-Parisian space with crowded tables as it is for its authentic French bistro cuisine at reasonable prices. A regular following of Bucktown locals and foodies is willing to wait for a table here. French menu. Dinner. Closed Sun; holidays. Bar. Casual attire. Reservations recommended. **$$**

★ ★ MARCHE (156) (MAP D)
833 W Randolph St (60607)
Phone 312/226-8399
Fax 312/226-4169
www.marche-chicago.com

Located along restaurant row in the West Loop, Marche serves imaginative versions of classic French bistro fare in a nightclub-like setting. Vibrant paintings and ultra-modern furnishings give the restaurant an eclectic feel and may make you feel as if you have stepped onto the set of *Moulin Rouge*. Sit back with a glass of Veuve and enjoy the theatrical surroundings of this grand French brasserie. French bistro menu. Lunch, dinner. Closed holidays. Bar. Casual attire. Valet parking. Outdoor seating. **$$$**

★★ MAS 157 (MAP E)

1670 W Division St (60622)
Phone 773/276-8700

This Wicker Park favorite is a good place for a Nuevo Latino feast, a wonderful alternative to more familiar cuisines. The fresh, spicy, and creative fare is best paired with a caipirinha, batida, or mojito to get, literally, in the spirit. Exposed brick and tile and an open kitchen set a hip yet earthy mood. Latin menu. Dinner. Bar. Casual attire. Outdoor seating. **$$$**

★★★ MERITAGE 158 (MAP E)

2118 N Damen Ave (60647)
Phone 773/235-6434
www.meritagecafe.com

For a storefront Bucktown restaurant, Meritage aims high, dishing seafood-focused fare inspired by the cuisine and wines of the Pacific Northwest. Pacific Rim influences edge into seared salmon with taro pancake and Japanese spiced roast scallops. Meat lovers and red wine drinkers are ably served with seared lamb and duck confit. Though the spacious outdoor patio is enclosed and heated in winter, only a canopy cloisters the space in summer, making Meritage one of the city's best open-air eateries. American menu. Dinner, Sun brunch. Closed holidays. Bar. Casual attire. Outdoor seating. **$$$**

★★★ MIRAI SUSHI 159 (MAP E)

2020 W Division St (60622)
Phone 773/862-8500
Fax 773/862-8510
www.miraisushi.com

Wicker Park's funky-hip sushi hotspot is serious about sushi. Offering more than just your everyday maki and nigiri, Mirai ups the ante on sushi (fish is flown in daily, and some selections are still swimming), sake (a generous list), and Japanese culinary creativity (with an intriguing menu items and specials). The bilevel restaurant boasts a bright, smoke-free main-floor dining area and sushi bar, your best bet for experiencing the sushi chef's specials; the upstairs sake bar is dark and seductive, with a choice of barstools, tables, or sleek lounge furniture, with deejay music on weekends. Sushi menu. Dinner. Closed holidays. Bar. Casual attire. Outdoor seating. **$$$**

★ ★ ★ MOD 160 (MAP E)
1520 N Damen Ave (60622)
Phone 773/252-1500
Don't let the trippy, geometric-acrylic décor fool you; the food here is serious enough, as evidenced by the commitment to seasonal ingredients and composed plate presentations. The American fare, wine list, and background music could all be described as intelligently eclectic, making MOD a hit with both the hipster Wicker Park crowd and more seasoned, suited-up diners with a sense of adventure. A happening bar scene, Sunday brunch, and seasonal outdoor dining add to the restaurant's appeal. American menu. Dinner, Sun brunch. Bar. Outdoor seating. **$$**

★ ★ ★ NINE 161 (MAP D)
440 W Randolph St (60606)
Phone 312/575-9900
www.n9ne.com
A scene-setter in the West Loop, this Vegas-worthy spot blends sophistication and sizzle and backs it up with serious American steakhouse fare, a central champagne and caviar bar, and great people watching. Equally suited to business and social dining, Nine is a one-stop evening out, with a large bar/lounge area and another late-night upstairs lounge, the Ghost Bar. American menu. Lunch, dinner. Closed Sun; holidays. Bar. Casual attire. **$$$**

★ NORTHSIDE CAFE 162 (MAP E)
1635 N Damen Ave (60647)
Phone 773/384-3555
Fax 773/384-6337
The perfect place for people watching in the hip Bucktown neighborhood, or for a late-night snack (the kitchen is open until 2 am), the Northside Cafe is a local favorite for standard—but tasty—bar food, such as burgers, salads, and sandwiches. Summer is especially popular here, when the patio opens up and patrons can enjoy the great weather while sipping on one of Northside's famous frozen margaritas. American menu. Lunch, dinner. Closed Thanksgiving, Dec 24-25. Bar. Casual attire. Outdoor seating. **$$**

★★ OHBA 163 (MAP E)
2049 W Division St (60622)
Phone 773/772-2727
Fax 773/862-8500
www.ohbalounge.com
A spin-off of nearby sushi hotspot Mirai (see), this minimal-chic hipster haunt on the Division Street restaurant row puts out lovely presentations of contemporary "world cuisine" with an Asian accent. Expect luxury ingredients and unusual preparations, plus an extensive sake list, including flights and sake-based cocktails. Eclectic/ International menu. Lunch, dinner. Closed Mon; holidays. Bar. Casual attire. Outdoor seating. **$$**

★★★ ONE SIXTYBLUE 164 (MAP D)
160 N Loomis (60607)
Phone 312/850-0303
Fax 312/829-3046
www.onesixtyblue.com
Award-winning, haute contemporary cuisine and sleek, high-styled décor by famed designer Adam Tihany define this adult, urban dining experience in the West Loop. Bold American fare with French roots is at home in the contemporary yet comfortable dining room, done in dark wood and citrus hues with discreet lighting and great sightlines. The open kitchen and dramatic wine storage are focal points. A cocoa bar offers sinful chocolate creations; the chic lounge is a hot cocktail spot. The buzz over former Chicago Bull Michael Jordan's partnership is a mere whisper now that his limelight has dimmed. American menu. Dinner. Closed Sun; holidays. Bar. Casual attire. **$$$**

★ PARTHENON 165 (MAP D)
314 S Halsted St (60661)
Phone 312/726-2407
Fax 312/726-3203
www.theparthenon.com
A Greektown landmark, this long-standing, family-run favorite is known for its convivial taverna atmosphere and solid renditions of moderately priced, classic Greek fare (flaming cheese and lamb dishes are standouts)—and the free valet parking is a bonus. Greek menu. Lunch, dinner. Closed Thanksgiving, Dec 25. Bar. Children's menu. Casual attire. Valet parking. **$$**

★ PIECE **166** (MAP E)
1927 W North Ave (60622)
Phone 773/772-4422
Chicago may be the home of deep-dish pizza, but you'll never find it on the menu at this Wicker Park pizzeria. The only pizza served here is the East Coast-style thin-crust variety (one of the co-owners hails from Connecticut). Diners can order one of Piece's specialty pizzas or create their own using one of the bases—red, white, or plain—and a variety of ingredients ranging from the traditional tomatoes and mushrooms to the more adventurous clams and bacon. And what's pizza without beer? Ten regional microbrews and seven house-brewed beers are on hand to wash it all down. Pizza. Lunch, dinner, late-night. Bar. Casual attire. **$**

★ POT PAN **246** (MAP E)
1750 W North Ave (60622)
Phone 773/862-6990
Fax 773/862-6993
This simple noodle house is a favorite with Wicker Park/Bucktown locals, who enjoy the homey décor and inexpensive Thai food. Pot Pan is known for its outstanding Panang curry as well as its great spring rolls. Thai menu. Lunch, dinner. **$**

★ ★ RED LIGHT **167** (MAP D)
820 W Randolph St (60607)
Phone 312/733-8880
www.redlight-chicago.com
Asian fusion in an avant-garde, fantasy atmosphere defines this restaurant row favorite. Renowned chef Jackie Shen has taken over the kitchen, which produces fresh, creative combinations of Chinese, Thai, Japanese, and American ingredients and preparations. This hot-spot can be very noisy during prime time. Asian menu. Lunch, dinner. Closed Jan 1, Thanksgiving, Dec 25. Bar. Casual attire. Valet parking. Outdoor seating. **$$**

★ ★ ★ RODAN **168** (MAP E)
1530 N Milwaukee Ave (60622)
Phone 773/276-7036
A funky, globe-trotting Wicker Parker, Rodan unites the foods of South America and Asia on its menu. Graze from gingered swordfish and shrimp rolls back west to adobo Cornish hen and fish tacos with

mango salsa. Somewhere in between lies the tasty wasabi tempura fries. Go casual to Rodan, and go late-night if you're looking for a hip lounge. As the night progresses, the lights come down, the music comes up, and the bar fills with revelers. South American, Southeast Asian menu. Dinner, late-night. Bar. Casual attire. **$$**

★★ROSEBUD 169 (MAP D)

1500 W Taylor St (60607)
Phone 312/942-1117
www.rosebudrestaurants.com
The Taylor Street original of this expanding family of old-school Italian restaurants is a Little Italy tradition, revered for its boisterous Sinatra-swagger ambience; clubby, carved wood décor; and giant portions with inevitable doggie bags. There's a large bar area for waiting during peak periods. Italian menu. Lunch, dinner. Bar. Casual attire. Outdoor seating. **$$**

★★RUSHMORE 170 (MAP D)

1023 W Lake St (60607)
Phone 312/421-8845; toll-free 888/874-8719
www.rushmore-chicago.com
American regional food shines at Rushmore in the trendy West Loop. The kitchen plucks comfort food classics from around the country to include smoked cheddar macaroni and cheese, cornmeal-crusted fried chicken, and fish and chips fancied up to include trout and matchstick potatoes. In contrast to the homey food, the atmosphere leans toward the contemporary, providing a window to the front-line cooks. American menu. Lunch, dinner. Closed Sun. Bar. Casual attire. **$$**

★★SANTORINI 171 (MAP D)

800 W Adams St (60607)
Phone 312/829-8820
Fax 312/829-6263
www.santoriniseafood.com
This Greektown seafood specialist represents an oasis of calm amid its more boisterous companions on the neighborhood's busy strip. Authentic, fresh fish (especially the whole-grilled offerings) and the airy, Mediterranean seaside atmosphere with whitewashed walls transport patrons to the island of the same name. Greek menu. Lunch, dinner. Closed Thanksgiving, Dec 25. Bar. Children's menu. Casual attire. Valet parking. Outdoor seating. **$$**

taste of chicago

What started out more than 20 years ago as a way to sample cuisines from some of the city's best-known restaurants has become an all-out food fest and Fourth of July celebration that attracts more than 3.5 million visitors a year. At this ten-day event, which features booths from more than 50 area vendors, you can stick to Taste favorites—Lou Malnati's pizza, Eli's cheesecake, Robinson's ribs and giant turkey drumsticks, and sautéed goat meat and plantains from Vee-Vee's African restaurant—or indulge in more refined specialties, like coconut lime sorbet, duck with lingonberries, grilled lobster tail, and alligator on a stick. In addition to food, you'll find free live music by big-name headliners, amusement park rides, and even a parent helper tent with free diapers. The crowds can get oppressive, so the earlier in the day you go, the better; don't forget to bring water, sunscreen, patience, and, perhaps, some wetnaps. Also try to buy food tickets in advance to avoid long lines. Late June-early July. *Grant Park. Phone 312/774-6630 (Chicago Office of Tourism). www.cityofchicago.org.*

★ ★ **SOUK** (MAP E)
1552 N Milwaukee Ave (60622)
Phone 773/227-1818
Fax 773/278-1408
www.soukrestaurant.com
Stepping into the exotic surroundings of Souk (Arabic for "market-place") is like entering another world—tile artwork, beads, candles, leather-topped tables, and long, plush banquettes decorate the cozy dining room. It is the perfect atmosphere in which to dine on a menu that reflects all cultures of the Mediterranean, including Turkey, Greece, Morocco, and Egypt. Familiar dishes like hummus and baba ghanoush are among the selections, as are some not-so-familiar dishes like toshka and keba. Entertainment, which includes jazz and belly dancing, is offered weekly and perfect to watch while enjoying a post-dinner shisha (water pipe),filled with fruit tobacco. Mediterranean menu. Dinner. Bar. Casual attire. Reservations recommended. **$$**

★ ★ ★ ★ SPRING 🔵173 (MAP E)
2039 W North Ave (60647)
Phone 773/395-7100
www.springrestaurant.net

You don't expect it of the bohemian Wicker Park surroundings, but Spring is one of the city's most sophisticated foodies. Chef Shawn McClain has a deft touch with seafood, the specialty here prepared with Asian touches. Artistic but unfussy dishes change seasonally but might include tuna tartare with quail egg or cod in crab and sweet pea sauce. Lodged in a former bathhouse with the white ceramic wall tiles to prove it, Spring faces east for inspiration, greeting diners in the foyer with a Zen-inspired rock garden. American menu. Dinner. Closed holidays; early Jan. Bar. Casual attire. **$$$**

★ ★ SUSHI WABI 🔵174 (MAP D)
842 W Randolph St (60607)
Phone 312/563-1224
Fax 312/563-9579
www.sushiwabi.com

Chicago's first in a wave of hipster sushi bars draws a fashionable crowd to the West Loop market district for the fresh fish, industrial-chic atmosphere, and late-night deejay music. The clubby (noisy) scene is secondary to the seafood, and savvy sushi lovers know that reservations are a must. Japanese, sushi menu. Lunch, dinner. Closed holidays. Bar. Casual attire. Reservations recommended. **$$**

★ TOAST 🔵175 (MAP E)
2046 N Damen Ave (60647)
Phone 773/772-5600

This popular breakfast and lunch spot gives classic favorites a trendy twist: eggs Benedict are served with a decadent white truffle hollandaise, and a mountain of French toast is stuffed with strawberries and mascarpone cheese. Prices are reasonable, and the atmosphere is fun, with vintage toasters decorating the small, colorful dining room. American menu. Breakfast, lunch. Closed holidays. Casual attire. **$**

★ TRE KRONOR 176 (MAP G)
3258 W Foster Ave (60625)
Phone 773/267-9888
Fax 773/478-3058
Although it's out of the way, Tre Kronor warrants a trip to the
North Park neighborhood for its sincere welcome and delicious
Scandinavian comfort food. The family-run storefront serves meals
all day, from muesli and Danish blue cheese omelettes at breakfast
to Swedish meatball sandwiches at lunch and roast pork with figs at
dinner. The servers are cheerful, as is the folk-art décor. Scandanavian
menu. Breakfast, lunch, dinner. Closed holidays. Casual attire. **$$**

★ ★ TUSCANY 177 (MAP D)
1014 W Taylor St (60612)
Phone 312/829-1990
Fax 312/829-8023
www.stefanirestaurants.com
With its cozy dining area, wood-burning ovens, and rustic atmo-
sphere, this upscale Little Italy eatery is reminiscent of an Italian
trattoria. The northern Italian menu features homemade pastas
and gourmet pizzas, as well as a selection of grilled items like pork,
chicken, duck, veal, and steak. And who can forget dessert? Classic
Italian sweets like gelato, tiramisu, and cannoli are among the ways
to end your meal. Italian menu. Lunch, dinner. Closed Jan 1, Dec 25.
Bar. Valet parking. **$$**

★ ★ VIVO 178 (MAP D)
838 W Randolph St (60607)
Phone 312/733-3379
Fax 312/733-4436
www.vivo-chicago.com
With the distinction of having pioneered the now-booming Randolph
Street restaurant row, Vivo continues to draw a hip crowd for its
groovy, contemporary grotto atmosphere (exposed brick, candlelight,
and piles of wine bottles) and straightforward Italian fare. The
antipasti spread near the entrance is a welcoming, authentic touch.
Italian menu. Lunch, dinner. Closed Jan 1, Dec 25. Bar. Casual attire.
Valet parking. Outdoor seating. **$$**

★ ★ ★ WEST TOWN TAVERN   (MAP D)

1329 W Chicago Ave (60622)
Phone 312/666-6175
www.westtowntavern.com

Beloved Chicago chef Susan Goss and her wine-knowing husband Drew Goss run West Town Tavern, an upscale comfort foodie in a handsome brick-walled storefront that encourages repeats with genuine warmth. If it's on the menu, start with the beer cheese ball, the kind of spreadable cheddar last seen on New Year's Eve in the late 1960s. Entrées include maple-cured pork chops, steak in zinfandel sauce, and duck confit. Desserts finish charmingly via the classed-up s'mores with homemade marshmallows. West Town's wine selection roams far and wide on the interesting and largely affordable list. American menu. Dinner. Closed Sun. Bar. Casual attire. Outdoor seating. **$$**

★ WISHBONE   (180) (MAP D)

1001 W Washington Blvd (60607)
Phone 312/850-2663
Fax 312/850-4332
www.wishbonechicago.com

Casual Southern dishes at reasonable prices in colorful settings filled with faux-outdoor art comprise the winning combination at Wishbone. Lunches and dinners serve up bean-based hoppin' John, blackened catfish, and shrimp and grits. Breakfast offers plenty of unusual choices, such as crab cakes, to round out the egg offerings. Be an early bird at any meal to expect to dine here on a weekend; throngs of diners are drawn to both this location in the West Loop and in Lakeview (3300 N Lincoln). American menu. Lunch, dinner, brunch. Closed holidays. Children's menu. **$$**

North Shore

Sprawling homes, beautifully landscaped parks, and scenic drives characterize the cities and towns north of Chicago, situated along Lake Michigan's shoreline. Along the lake, find public beaches (with adjacent parking typically available only to local residents) and Sheridan Road—one of the nation's top drives past mansions that will make your jaw drop. Venture inland to browse upscale shops or dine in the local eateries of these sleepy, tranquil communities. Big-city enthusiasts will experience less withdrawal if they venture just north of Chicago to nearby Evanston—a diverse city featuring a large downtown business district and Northwestern University. Attractions farther north include the Baha'i House of Worship, Westfield Shoppingtown Old Orchard, the Charles Gates Dawes House, and the Chicago Botanic Garden.

Many of Chicago's elite live along the North Shore, the most famous such resident being basketball superstar and Highland Park hom-eowner Michael Jordan. During the 1980s and '90s, writer/director John Hughes returned to the northern suburbs again and again to film such comedies as *The Breakfast Club, Ferris Bueller's Day Off, She's Having a Baby,* and *Home Alone.*

Evanston

Evanston sits immediately north of Chicago, occupying an enviable expanse of land along Lake Michigan. The city hosts the Fountain Square Art Festival early each summer, a well-attended gathering of artists who line up on the downtown streets to market their works, ranging from paintings and photographs to jewelry and hand blown glass. The home to Northwestern University, Evanston boasts a multitude of art galleries, theaters, shops, and restaurants. The community is serviced by the Purple Line of Chicago's famed "L" mass-transit system.

Restaurants in Evanston

★★★ CAMPAGNOLA (MAP H)
815 Chicago Ave (60202)
Phone 847/475-6100
Evanston proves that sophisticated dining does venture outside the Chicago city limits, and Campagnola is a fine example of this trend. Chef/owner Michael Altenberg's rustic but elegant menu features many seasonal organic ingredients. A knowledgeable waitstaff serves diners in two dining areas: a formal dining room upstairs and a more casual (and less pricey) trattoria downstairs. Italian menu. Dinner. Closed Mon; holidays. Reservations recommended. Valet parking.
$$$

★ CARMEN'S (MAP H)
1012 Church St (60201)
Phone 847/328-0031
In a college town, you can't go wrong opening a pizza restaurant. Carmen's, a longstanding Evanston hit, assured its success by offering a range of pizzas, including classic stuffed versions, deep-dish pies, and more daring renditions such as pesto pizza. Extending its appeal to families and business folk in addition to campus types, Carmen's keeps shop in a modest but cozy, two-story den warmed by wood beams and a fireplace. Salads and substantial pastas round out the offerings. Pizza. Dinner. Closed holidays. Bar. **$**

★★ THE DINING ROOM AT KENDALL COLLEGE (MAP H)
2408 Orrington Ave (60201)
Phone 847/866-1399
www.kendall.edu
Students at Evanston's Kendall College, which emphasizes culinary arts and hotel management, staff both the front and back of the

house in the campus' intimate Dining Room. Menus change frequently, but the cooking remains remarkably accomplished in dishes like ostrich filet with dried cherry risotto, braised lamb shank with rapini, and lobster risotto. Spy the kitchen staff at work from behind plate-glass windows while you dine. Expect amiable but not polished service; those who work the floor are in training at the stoves too. The price is right, with most entrées under $20. American menu. Lunch, dinner. Closed Sun; holidays. Reservations recommended. **$$**

★ ★ DON'S FISHMARKET (MAP I)
9335 Skokie Blvd, Skokie (60077)
Phone 847/677-3424
Fax 847/679-5849
www.donsfishmarket.com
More than 25 years old, this subtly nautical-themed restaurant and tavern boasts a friendly staff and reasonably priced fare. The stars of the menu are—you guessed it—a variety of fresh seafood selections, from Chilean sea bass to whitefish from the Great Lakes to Alaskan king crab legs. Steaks and chops are available for those who prefer to dine off the land. Seafood menu. Lunch, dinner. Closed Jan 1, Thanksgiving, Dec 25. Bar. Children's menu. Casual attire. **$$**

★ ★ JILLY'S CAFE (MAP H)
2614 Green Bay Rd (60201)
Phone 847/869-7636
Romance is on the menu at this small café. Rising above its storefront confines, Jilly's manages to affect a French country inn where bonhomie reigns among close-set tables. The kitchen produces classic but substantial meals, with raves for escargot, roast pork tenderloin, and seared veal medallions. Service is accomplished, courses paced. Try the prix fixe Sunday brunch for a leisurely indulgence. American menu. Dinner, Sun brunch. Closed Mon; holidays. **$$**

★ LAS PALMAS 186 (MAP H)
817 University Pl (60201)
Phone 847/328-2555
The Evanston outpost of Las Palmas—there are several others in and around Chicago—proffers authentic and familiar Mexican fare at moderate, crowd-pleasing prices. More traditional dishes, including grilled shrimp, skirt steak tacos (tacos al carbon), chiles rellenos, and mole enchiladas, are supplemented by the popular fajitas. Rustic wooden tables under beamed ceilings provide fiesta-ready and family-friendly seating. Mexican menu. Lunch, dinner. Closed Thanksgiving, Dec 25. Bar. **$$**

★ LUCKY PLATTER (MAP H)

514 Main St (60202)
Phone 847/869-4064
Lucky Platter's kitschy flea-market décor—you can't miss the paint-by-numbers artwork on the walls, retro lamps, and mounted deer head—creates a lighthearted atmosphere for border-busting fare. The menu ranges from all-American pot roast to Jamaican jerk chicken, with forays into India and Thailand. At peak meal times (read: week-ends), you may be lucky to get a table at the popular Platter, so plan accordingly. Service is often amateurish but usually well-meaning. Eclectic/International menu. Breakfast, lunch, dinner. **$$**

★ MERLE'S #1 BARBECUE (MAP H)

1727 Benson St (60201)
Phone 847/475-7766
Merle's takes a Southern tour through St. Louis, Memphis, and Texas, serving up slow-cooked barbecue in down-home digs. The regional menu offers both wet (with sauce) and dry-spice-rubbed ribs, pulled beef sandwiches, and sides, including Texas fries, baked beans, and North Carolina red rice. With a crowd in tow, try the generous "barn-yard" sampler platter. Country music memorabilia and Elvis photos contribute to the roadhouse aura. Southwestern menu. Dinner. Closed Thanksgiving, Dec 25. Bar. Children's menu. **$$**

★ ★ NEW JAPAN (MAP H)

1322 Chicago Ave (60201)
Phone 847/475-5980
Both sushi lovers and sushi snubbers find common ground in New Japan, a neighborhood favorite with a large following of regulars. Aficionados tout its reasonable prices and high quality in both its raw fish selections as well as its often-French-accented cooked dishes, including steak teriyaki, stir-fried vegetables, curry rice, and whole salmon. Genuine warmth distinguishes the staffers here. Japanese, French menu. Lunch, dinner. Closed Mon; holidays. **$$**

★ ★ ★ OCEANIQUE (MAP H)
505 Main St (60202)
Phone 847/864-3435
www.oceanique.com
As the name suggests, the focus of this softly lit restaurant is seafood. Dishes are intelligently prepared and include a stellar bouillabaisse of squid, salmon, and shrimp in a saffron-scented broth. The room, relaxed and social, is filled with residents and academics of the Northwestern University town. French, American menu. Dinner. Closed Sun; holidays. **$$$**

★ ★ PETE MILLER'S STEAKHOUSE (MAP H)
1557 Sherman Ave (60201)
Phone 847/328-0399
Evanstonians acclaim the longstanding Pete Miller's for both excellent food and 1940s-vintage décor. Dim lighting, wood and brass accents, and old black-and-white street photography conjure another era. Bask in it over steakhouse classics such as bone-in ribeye, double baked potatoes, lobster tail, and, to finish, bananas foster. Superior hamburgers satisfy simpler tastes. Stick around after 8:30 pm, when the live jazz band strikes up. Steak menu. Lunch, dinner. Closed July 4, Thanksgiving, Dec 25. Bar. Valet parking. **$$**

★ PRAIRIE MOON (MAP H)
1502 Sherman Ave (60201)
Phone 847/864-UEAT
Fax 847/864-3302
www.prairiemoonrestaurant.com
This uncluttered, modern dining room in central Evanston (conveniently located across from a parking garage) celebrates American diversity. Regional festival posters adorn the walls, and a different festival is featured each month, with food and drink specials from the region to match. The menu, which offers both small and big plates, is stocked with regional specialties like Chesapeake blue crabcakes, Colorado brook trout, and Texas sheet cake. American menu. Lunch, dinner, late-night, Sun brunch. Closed Thanksgiving, Dec 25. Bar. Children's menu. Casual attire. Outdoor seating. **$$**

★ ★ ★ ★ ★ TRIO (MAP H)

1625 Hinman Ave (60201)
Phone 847/733-8746
Fax 847/733-8748
www.trio-restaurant.com

Located in a quiet little inn just north of Chicago, Trio offers guests the opportunity to dine on a unique menu of avant-garde American fare. The kitchen honors fresh, seasonal ingredients with sauces, vinaigrettes, and purees that support and accent each ingredient's texture and flavor. The kitchen works hard at being responsibly creative—you'll taste a dish and be struck with wonder and delight rather than fear. The four- and eight-course tasting menus are both excellent options for experiencing Trio's innovative repertoire, while the 20-course "Tour de Force" offers what the restaurant calls "the ultimate in culinary ecstacy." The dining room strikes a perfect balance of rustic charm and urban style with a brick fireplace, warm weathered walls, and finely appointed tabletops, making it a perfect spot for dinner with friends, family, or your significant other. American menu. Dinner. Closed Mon-Tues; holidays. Reservations recommended. **$$$$**

★ ★ VA PENSIERO (MAP H)

1566 Oak Ave (60201)
Phone 847/475-7779
Fax 847/475-7825

One of best Italian restaurants on the North Shore, Va Pensiero warrants special-occasion dining. The airy room posted by Roman columns creates an elegant setting for sophisticated preparations such as olive oil-braised tuna, pesto tiger prawns, and lobster ravioli, as well as classics including carpaccio, risotto, and lamb chops. Despite the upscale trappings, Va Pensiero, inside the Margarita European Inn, is family friendly. Servers are adept at guiding you through the mostly Italian wine list. Italian menu. Dinner. Closed holidays. Bar. Outdoor seating. **$$**

Highland Park

This lakefront community is located 23 miles north of Chicago and 23 miles west of O'Hare International Airport. Browse the city's pricey upscale boutiques, enjoy free summer music concerts in Port Clinton Square, or dine in one of the local restaurants, featuring varied cuisine—many with outdoor seating in summer. Don't miss a warm-weather concert under the stars at Ravinia Festival, which runs from May through late September.

Restaurants in Highland Park

★ ★ CAFE CENTRAL (MAP G)

455 Central Ave (60035)
Phone 847/266-7878
Fax 847/266-7373
www.cafecentral.com
This suburban eatery, located in the heart of downtown Highland Park, is within easy walking distance of area shops. The restaurant serves up French cuisine in a casual setting. Sample locally acclaimed dishes such as risotto or poached chicken salad, as well as selections ranging from quiche and salads to sandwiches and pasta. French menu. Lunch, dinner. Closed Mon; Jan 1, July 4, Dec 25. Bar. Children's menu. Casual attire. Outdoor seating. **$$**

★ ★ ★ CARLOS' (MAP G)

429 Temple Ave (60035)
Phone 847/432-0770
www.carlos-restaurant.com
Owned by husband and wife hosts Carlos and Debbie Nieto, Carlos' is a uniquely elegant and intimate restaurant, with mismatched vintage china, fresh flowers, and deep, fabric-covered banquettes. For more than 20 years, the Nietos have been graciously welcoming guests celebrating anniversaries, birthdays, weddings, and just about every other excuse they can make up for dining here. While the Nietos are generous hosts, it is not only their welcome that makes this homey dining room so popular. In all fairness, the gifted chefs also deserve some credit. Carlos' is known for its stellar haute cuisine served in classic French style: entrées arrive topped with silver domes, which the restaurant's charming staff lift in unison on the count of "One, two, three, voilà!" The wine list is as impressive as the cuisine, with more than 3,500 international selections to choose from. *Secret Inspector's Notes: If you are seeking "fusion cuisine" or innovative, unrecognizable entrées, Carlos' is not the place for you. But if you*

desire a classic destination for elegant dining and proper service, away from the noise and traffic of downtown Chicago, this is the perfect match. French menu. Dinner. Closed Tues; holidays. Jacket required. Reservations recommended. Valet parking. **$$$**

★ MICHAEL'S RESTAURANT   (MAP G)

1879 Second St (60035)
Phone 847/432-3338
www.michaelshotdogs.com

Savor some of Chicago's finest hot dogs at this longstanding institution in central Highland Park. Diners travel from Chicago and the surrounding suburbs to enjoy high-end fast food served in a colorful, casual setting that's perfect for families. Lunch and dinner entrées include potatoes with every manner of fixing; a wide variety of wraps; a create-your-own salad bar; pita pockets; grilled items; and sundaes and other sweet confections. A children's menu downsizes several options to suit smaller appetites. Don't miss a char dog, burger, or chicken breast sandwich, and save room for an order of cheddar fries. American menu. Lunch, dinner. Children's menu. No credit cards accepted. **$**

ravinia festival

The summer home of the Chicago Symphony Orchestra is also the summer playground for thousands of Chicago's music lovers. This former amusement park–turned classical music venue–turned classy outdoor extravaganza features programming that spans the musical and artistic spectrum, from Bonnie Raitt and Los Lobos to Tony Bennett, Herbie Hancock, and Itzhak Perlman. Special programs include Jazz in June, the Young Artists series, and Kids Concerts. While there is a 3,200-seat, open-air pavilion and two indoor venues for chamber music and smaller concerts, the majority of festival-goers prefer the lawn, where you can relax with a picnic and listen via the excellent sound system. Plus, it's fun to watch the one-upmanship of the surrounding picnickers; china, crystal, and candelabras are not uncommon. Out-of-towners can still enjoy the lawn and not bring a thing: the park offers five restaurants, a picnic catering facility, chair rentals, and wine kiosks. *418 Sheridan Rd, Highland Park (60035). Phone 847/266-5100. www.ravinia.org.*

Highwood

Sandwiched between Highland Park and Lake Forest, this suburban community along Chicago's North Shore is known both for its numerous restaurants and its close association to Fort Sheridan, a former army base. Local attractions include Everts Park, the Robert McClory Bicycle Path, and the 18-hole Lake County Forest Preserve golf course at the Fort Sheridan Club. All are open to the public.

Restaurants in Highwood

★★ DEL RIO (MAP G)
228 Green Bay Rd (60040)
Phone 847/432-4608

A genuine bite of Highwood's past as an Italian immigrant enclave, the family-run Del Rio has been dishing heaping portions of Italian classics since the 1930s. The menu breaks no new ground, but that's just the way fans like it, pouring in for generous helpings of lasagna, sausage and peppers, veal parmigiana, chicken cacciatore, and homemade pastas. Italian maps and menus decorate the walls of the homey and usually crowded eatery. Italian menu. Dinner. Closed holidays. Bar. **$$$**

★★★ FROGGY'S (MAP G)
306 Green Bay Rd (60040)
Phone 847/433-7080
Fax 847/433-6852
www.froggyscatering.com

This cheery bistro offers country French cuisine at reasonable prices (try the bargain prix fixe menu), with regional specialties like onion soup, coq au vin, and rabbit casserole rounding out the menu. The nice-sized wine list features a number of red and white Burgundies, Bordeaux, and Champagnes, and decadent cakes and carry-out items can be purchased from the adjacent bakery. French menu. Lunch, dinner. Closed Sun; holidays. Bar. **$$**

★ ★ ★ GABRIEL'S 200 (MAP G)
310 Green Bay Rd (60040)
Phone 847/433-0031
www.egabriels.com

Chef/owner Gabriel Viti, formerly of Carlos' in Highland Park (see), turns out complex French-Italian dishes from his open kitchen in his namesake restaurant. Entrées range from grilled veal porterhouse to roasted Maine lobster with baby bok choy and ginger butter sauce, with seasonal specials and a degustation menu available. Attentive service characterizes this upscale-casual restaurant, whose décor features handpainted tiles and linen-topped tables. French, Italian menu. Dinner. Closed Sun-Mon; holidays. Bar. Reservations recommended. Valet parking. Outdoor seating. **$$$$**

Lake Forest

Lake Forest has long been regarded as an enclave of affluence and prestige. Here, sprawling estates spread out upon bluffs overlooking Lake Michigan. Thirty miles north of Chicago, Lake Forest is the home to Lake Forest College, as well as Halas Hall, the headquarters for the legendary Chicago Bears. Lake Forest's central business district, Market Square, was listed on the National Register of Historic Places in 1979.

Restaurants in Lake Forest

★ ★ BANK LANE BISTRO 201 (MAP G)
670 Bank Ln (60045)
Phone 847/234-8802
Posters of Paris and large picture windows framing Lake Forest's historic downtown entertain diners at Bank Lane Bistro. Although the menu changes frequently, you can count on such French bistro classics as escargot, braised lamb shank, and roast pork, as well as crispy pizzas from the wood-burning oven. Service is assured, but with prices on the high side, fans recommend Bank Lane on occasion rather than regularly. French menu. Lunch, dinner. Closed Sun. Bar. Casual attire. Outdoor seating. **$$$**

★ ★ ★ THE ENGLISH ROOM 202 (MAP G)
255 E Illinois St (60045)
Phone 847/234-2280
Set inside the historic Deer Path Inn, which opened in 1929 and has been a destination for weekend getaways and fine dining ever since, The English Room is an elegant, traditional dining room. The conservative dinner menu includes options like lobster bisque, roasted rack of lamb, and Dover sole; lunch options are a bit more varied and adventurous. The Sunday Champagne brunch is especially treasured here, with its carving stations, ample seafood selections, and sinful desserts. American menu. Buffet, lunch, dinner, Sun brunch. Bar. Children's menu. Jacket required. Outdoor seating. **$$$**

★★ SOUTH GATE CAFE (MAP G)

655 Forest Ave (60045)
Phone 847/234-8800
www.southgatecafe.com

Peering over namesake South Gate Square, this upscale café serves American food with a passport to the country's food-centric regions as well as more exotic cultures. Options range from Asian pork satay to Norwegian salmon, beef tenderloin with mushrooms, and, as a last act, bread pudding made with Kentucky bourbon. The environs are somewhat austere, but servers lend warmth. The leafy outdoor patio generates North Shore destination traffic, so arrive early or expect to wait. American menu. Lunch, dinner. Closed holidays. Bar. **$$**

Wilmette

Immediately north of Evanston and 15 miles from downtown Chicago, Wilmette possesses an idyllic location on Lake Michigan's shoreline. Visually, this community has changed little over the years, with old-fashioned lampposts standing alongside tree-lined brick streets. The Wilmette Park District manages 19 public parks, including the popular Gillson Beach. Wilmette is home to the Baha'i House of Worship, a domed architectural marvel that was placed on the National Register of Historic Places in 1978.

Restaurants in Wilmette

★ ★ BETISE (MAP G)

1515 N Sheridan Rd (60091)
Phone 847/853-1711

Great food, a convivial setting, and a casual vibe make Wilmette's Betise a popular North Shore stop. Classic bistro fare, including grilled fish and roasted meats, is supplemented by more daring specials. Although the restaurant is large, it's divided into smaller dining nooks, all posted with sketch art on the walls, carving out intimacy within the high-spirited setting. French bistro menu. Lunch, dinner, Sun brunch. Closed holidays. **$$**

★ ★ CONVITO ITALIANO (MAP G)

1515 N Sheridan Rd (60091)
Phone 847/251-3654
Fax 847/251-0123
www.convitoitaliano.com

Half gourmet import store, half casual trattoria, North Shore mainstay Convito Italiano earns applause for its light, seasonal Italian fare available both eat-in and take-out. Diners after the former are seated at marble tables in a skylit room for plates of homemade pasta, veal, and fish. Hit the deli side of the shop for frozen pastas and sauces, fresh salads, breads, desserts, and wine. Seasonal dining on the terrace offers glimpses of Lake Michigan. Italian menu. Dinner. Closed holidays. **$$**

★ WALKER BROTHERS ORIGINAL PANCAKE HOUSE (MAP H)

153 Green Bay Rd (60091)
Phone 847/251-6000
Fax 847/251-6191

If you love breakfast food, this north-suburban eatery is the place for you. Fresh, hot pancakes (chocolate chip, apple, banana . . .), hearty French toast, sweet and savory crepes, and a variety of omelet creations are a treat any time of the day or night. The quaint dining room, with mahogany tables and booths, Tiffany-style stained glass accents, and antique touches, attracts a considerable crowd for weekend breakfast and brunch. Other locations in Highland Park (620 Central Ave), Arlington Heights (825 Dundee Rd), Glenview (1615 Waukegan Rd), Lincolnshire (200 Marriott Dr), and Lake Zurich (767 S Rand Rd) are just as popular with scads of weekend brunchers. American menu. Breakfast, lunch, dinner. Closed Thanksgiving, Dec 25. Children's menu. **$**

Northern Suburbs

Chicago's northern suburbs are highly regarded for their charming downtowns, quiet residential neighborhoods, serene parks, and excellent schools. Chicago's bustling O'Hare Airport brings many travelers to this area of the city, as does the Donald E. Stephens Convention Center in nearby Rosemont. Downtown Chicago is easily accessible via the Metra railway system, which serves most northern suburbs, including Northbrook and Deerfield, to name but a couple of the stops. The suburban train stations serve as anchors to their communities, with numerous quaint shops and restaurants nearby.

Arlington Heights

Twenty-five miles northwest of Chicago, Arlington Heights possesses numerous public parks, tree-lined residential neighborhoods, and a thriving downtown possessing an eclectic mix of shops and restaurants. The community was founded as Dunton in 1836, later incorporating as Arlington Heights in 1887. Today, the village may be best known for Arlington Park, where the Arlington Million thoroughbred race is held annually in August.

Restaurants in Arlington Heights

★ ★ ★ LE TITI DE PARIS (MAP I)
1015 W Dundee Rd (60004)
Phone 847/506-0222
Fax 847/506-0474
www.letitideparis.com
With more than 800 selections, the wine list at this fantastic French restaurant is about as long as a Norman Mailer novel. Chefs Pierre Pollin and Michael Maddox serve marvelously innovative cuisine with nearly impeccable service. Signatures include such delights as sautéed salmon with cider sauce and Asian spiced duck. If you can, save room for one of the creatively presented desserts. French menu. Dinner. Closed Sun-Mon; holidays. Casual attire. **$$$**

★ ★ PALM COURT ❽ (MAP I)
1912 N Arlington Heights Rd (60004)
Phone 847/870-7770
Fax 847/870-8586
www.palmcourt.net
In an area that offers mostly chain restaurants, Palm Court is a refreshing option. Serving fresh seafood, steaks, lamb, and veal, the family-owned restaurant caters to businesspeople as well as to casual diners. Nightly live piano music adds a romantic touch to the good-sized bar area. American menu. Lunch (Mon-Fri), dinner. Closed July 4, Dec 25. Bar. Children's menu. Casual attire. Reservations recommended. **$$**

★★ RETRO BISTRO 209 (MAP I)

1746 W Golf Rd, Mount Prospect (60056)
Phone 847/439-2424

"Retro" aptly describes the décor and "Bistro" less specifically the food at the popular Retro Bistro. Black and white mid-20th-century posters on the walls create a noirish setting for the menu of French and American dishes. Options include crab cakes, roast rabbit, and grilled ostrich. The three-course prix fixe option is well priced. Despite its strip mall location, the atmospheric Retro proves to be a destination among suburbanites. French menu. Lunch, dinner. Closed Sun; holidays. Bar. Children's menu. **$$**

Glenview

Glenview is located 20 miles north of downtown Chicago, squeezed between Interstates 94 and 294. Following the Great Fire in 1871, the Chicago and Milwaukee Railroad was constructed to facilitate the rapid rebuilding of Chicago. The railroad passed through Glenview, then a sparsely populated agrarian community known as South Northfield. The introduction of the railroad spurred the community's growth, and today Glenview boasts numerous shops and restaurants, desirable residential neighborhoods, and exceptional public schools.

Restaurants in Glenview

★ ★ ★ MK NORTH ⬤210 (MAP G)
305 Happ Rd, Northfield (60093)
Phone 847/716-6500
www.mkchicago.com

Style meets substance at this northern outpost of Michael Kornick's mk, where refined yet real contemporary cuisine is offered in a perfectly compatible setting. The seasonal American food is clean and uncontrived, featuring such specialties as lobster bisque and salmon with Chinese mustard glaze. Knowledgeable service, a fine wine list (including private-label selections), and excellent desserts are all a part of the mk dining experience. Degustation menus are available, and the chic lounge area is perfect for a before-or-after glass of bubbly. American menu. Lunch, dinner. Closed Sun. Bar. Children's menu. Casual attire. Reservations recommended. Outdoor seating. **$$$**

★ PERIYALI GREEK TAVERNA ⬤211 (MAP I)
9860 Milwaukee Ave (60016)
Phone 847/296-2232
Fax 847/296-3250

The large outdoor seating area is the big draw at this authentic Greek restaurant at the south end of town, which used to be a Red Lobster. The equally sizable dining room is great for families and groups. Greek menu. Lunch, dinner. Closed Thanksgiving, Dec 25. Bar. Casual attire. Outdoor seating. **$$**

Libertyville

Marlon Brando, Helen Hayes, and Adlai Stevenson are a few of the famous personalities who have lived in Libertyville. The St. Mary of the Lake Theological Seminary (Roman Catholic) borders the town; there are four lakes near the village limits.

Restaurants in Libertyville

★ COUNTRY INN
RESTAURANT AT LAMBS FARM (MAP G)
14245 W Rockland Rd (60048)
Phone 847/362-5050
www.lambsfarm.org
Libertyville's down-on-the-farm breakfast and lunch specialist serves up a dose of country setting as a side to filling American fare made from scratch. Snag a table amid the antiques and dig into skillets and omelets at breakfast or homemade soups and comfort food specials, including barbecue ribs, fried chicken, and country ham, at lunch. House-baked breads come from the onsite bakery. American menu. Lunch, dinner, Sun brunch. Closed holidays. Children's menu. Reservations recommended. **$$**

★★ TAVERN IN THE TOWN (MAP I)
519 N Milwaukee Ave (60048)
Phone 847/367-5755
Along a stretch of near-wasteland suburbia sits this surprising bastion of Victorian charm. Guests dine in a romantic room of flowing curtains and brick and brass accents. American menu. Lunch, dinner. Closed Sun; holidays. Bar. **$$$**

Northbrook

The earliest European settlers in the Northbrook area were German immigrants who arrived after the construction of the Erie Canal in 1825. In 1901 the town was incorporated as Shermerville, in honor of one of the founding families. Brickyards played a major role in the prosperity and growth of the community. After the Chicago fire of 1871, brick manufacturing surpassed farming as a leading industry; 300,000 bricks per day were produced between 1915-1920. In 1923, Shermerville was renamed Northbrook in reference to the middle forks of the north branches of the Chicago River, which run through the town. Today, Northbrook is the headquarters of a number of major corporations.

Restaurants in Northbrook

★ ★ CEILING ZERO   214 (MAP G)

500 Anthony Trail (60062)
Phone 847/272-8111

Housed in a former airplane hangar once a part of Northbrook's airport, Ceiling Zero is well grounded in continental cuisine. The menu sticks to classics like lobster bisque, white fish almandine, peppercorn filet mignon and thick-cut pork chops. The reverent atmosphere and assured but formal service combine to make Ceiling Zero a special occasion eatery in old-school style. American menu. Lunch, dinner. Closed holidays. Bar. Casual attire. **$$**

★ FRANCESCO'S HOLE IN THE WALL   215 (MAP I)

254 Skokie Blvd (60062)
Phone 847/272-0155
Fax 847/482-0267

Tiny, thronged, and beloved, Francesco's trades in old-country neighborhood Italian fare, crowd-pleasing and well-priced dishes like chicken Vesuvio, veal chops, homemade pastas, and daily fish specials. Impatient and urgently hungry diners will be challenged by Francesco's inevitable waits for one of its mere 17 tables. But those in Francesco's fan camp rave for the cozy confines and friendly service. Bring cash, as credit cards are not accepted. Italian menu. Lunch, dinner. Closed Tues; holidays; also Jan. Casual attire. No credit cards accepted. **$$**

★ TONELLI'S 216 (MAP G)

1038 Waukegan Rd (60062)
Phone 847/272-4730
Fax 847/272-9370

Northbrook Italian Tonelli's serves up immigrant Italian-American food that takes you back to the old neighborhood. Go hungry for generous portions of lasagna, spaghetti with meatballs, baked mostaccioli, and, for the "dolce" course, tiramisu. Fans consider the pizza among the best in the northern suburbs. Portions are huge and prices reasonable, making Tonelli's a good value choice for families. Italian menu. Lunch, dinner. Closed Easter, Thanksgiving, Dec 25. Bar. Children's menu. Casual attire. Outdoor seating. **$$**

Rosemont

Rosemont sits to the immediate east of O'Hare International Airport, a 17-mile drive from downtown Chicago on the Kennedy Expressway (I-90/94). The community annually welcomes millions of visitors to the Donald E. Stephens Convention Center, the nation's tenth-largest meeting and convention center. The 19,000-seat Allstate Arena hosts professional sports and big-name musical acts, while the plush Rosemont Theater offers live entertainment in a more intimate environment. As would be expected given its location near O'Hare, Rosemont has a wide variety of hotels, adding up to more than 5,600 rooms available to visitors to the community.

Restaurants in Rosemont

★★ CAFE LA CAVE ⬤217 (MAP G)
2777 Mannheim Rd, Des Plaines (60018)
Phone 847/827-7818
Fax 847/827-3390
www.cafelacaverestaurant.com

O'Hare Airport neighbor Café La Cave divides patrons between a simulated grotto, favored by romance-seeking couples, and the elegant main dining room peopled by business diners on expense accounts. Both constituencies come for La Cave's classic continental menu starring steak Diane flamed tableside, delicate Dover sole, and rich bananas Foster, again flamed at your table. Prices reflect the high level of service practiced here. French menu. Dinner. Closed holidays. Bar. Casual attire. Valet parking. **$$$**

★★ CARLUCCI ⬤218 (MAP I)
6111 N River Rd (60018)
Phone 847/518-0990

Tucked inside an office building complex, Carlucci can be tough to find—look for the sign on River Road. The restaurant prides itself on its robust and simple Tuscan fare, with a variety of antipasti, hearty pasta dishes, and grilled meats rounding out the menu. More than 75 wines from Italy and California are available as well. Italian menu. Lunch, dinner. Closed holidays. Bar. Casual attire. Valet parking. Outdoor seating. **$$**

★ ★ ★ MORTON'S OF CHICAGO   (MAP I)

9525 W Bryn Mawr Ave (60018)
Phone 847/678-5155
www.mortons.com

This steakhouse chain, which originated in Chicago in 1978, appeals to serious meat lovers. With a selection of belt-busting carnivorous delights (like the house specialty, a 24-ounce porterhouse), as well as fresh fish, lobster, and chicken entrées, Morton's rarely disappoints. If you just aren't sure what you're in the mood for, the tableside menu presentation may help you decide. Here, main course selections are placed on a cart that's rolled to your table, where servers describe each item in detail. Steak menu. Dinner. Closed holidays. Bar. Valet parking. **$$**

🅳

★ ★ ★ NICK'S FISHMARKET   (MAP I)

10275 W Higgins Rd (60018)
Phone 847/298-8200
Fax 847/298-3755
www.nicksfishmarketchicago.com

An operation born in Hawaii in the mid-1960s, Nick's reveals its roots in Hawaiian fish specials and the "Maui Wowie" salad. Appetizers feature shellfish, sashimi, and caviar, followed by sole, salmon, and lobster entrées. This location, one of three in the metro area, features three enormous aquariums. The fish to pay attention to, however, are on the menu. Seafood menu. Dinner. Closed holidays. Bar. Children's menu. Casual attire. Valet parking. **$$$**

Wheeling

The Wheeling area was first occupied by the Potawatomi. Settlers arrived in 1833 and began farming the fertile prairie soil. In 1836, a stagecoach route was established along Milwaukee Avenue, which was the main northbound route out of Chicago. The first commercial enterprise was a tavern-hotel (1837), followed by the establishment of a brewery (1850) on the Des Plaines River.

Restaurants in Wheeling

★ ★ 94TH AERO SQUADRON   221 (MAP G)
1070 S Milwaukee Ave (Hwy 21) (60090)
Phone 847/459-3700
A thematic neighbor to the Palwaukee Airport next door, 94th Aero Squadron boosts its World War II fighter theme with a faux bombed-out interior and images of vintage planes. The something-for-everyone menu includes prime rib, steak, shrimp, and fish. Repeat customers say the food is nothing special, but it's group-friendly, and the Sunday brunch is worth the trek. American, steak menu. Dinner, Sun brunch. Bar. Children's menu. Outdoor seating. **$$**

★ ★ BOB CHINN'S CRAB HOUSE   222 (MAP I)
393 S Milwaukee Ave (Hwy 21) (60090)
Phone 847/520-3633
Fax 847/520-3944
www.bobchinns.com
Wheeling's high-volume draw Bob Chinn's draws diners from around Chicagoland—ranging from business groups to casually dressed clans—on the strength of its fresh seafood cooked umpteen ways.

---

long grove confectionary company

Take a tour of this family-owned confectionary that produces more than 300 sweet treats, in business since 1975. Learn how the chocolates are made, sample the products, and then purchase discounted goodies from the outlet store, open Monday through Saturday 9:30 am-5:30 pm and Sunday 11 am-4 pm. Tours are given Monday through Thursday at 9 am, 11 am, noon, and 1 pm; other times by appointment. Reservations are required. *333 Lexington Dr, Long Grove (60089). Phone 847/459-3100; toll-free 888/459-3100. www.longgrove.com.*

The best dishes are the simplest: cold or steamed crab legs, sautéed Hawaiian-caught fish, and raw bar oysters. House mai tais elevate spirits among those waiting for tables in the barny roadhouse decked in coastal décor. Seafood menu. Lunch, dinner. Closed Thanksgiving, Dec 25. Bar. Children's menu (dinner). Valet service. **$$**

★★ DON ROTH'S 223 (MAP I)
61 N Milwaukee Ave (Hwy 21) (60090)
Phone 847/537-5800
www.donroths.com
Period music and memorabilia from the original downtown Blackhawk restaurant in its 1920s, '30s, and '40s prime lend Chicago swagger to this Wheeling institution. Steaks, prime rib, and seafood center the menu, although many fans make the trip specifically for the famous "spinning salad bowl" rite in which waiters whip up salads tableside. The food is old-fashioned, but the genuine welcome is perennially fresh. Dinner. Steak menu. Closed Dec 25. Bar. Outdoor seating. **$$**

Western Suburbs

The western suburbs extend nearly 40 miles from Chicago's skyscrapers, beginning with progressive and historically rich Oak Park—the onetime home of Frank Lloyd Wright and Ernest Hemingway—and stretching out to charming communities along the Fox River such as St. Charles and Batavia. Driven by business development along the I-88 technology corridor, the adjacent suburbs of Naperville and Aurora have grown exponentially over the last 20 years, with their combined population now topping 280,000. A respite from the suburbs' increasing congestion can be found in Lisle, where the Morton Arboretum counts more than 3,600 outdoor plants thriving amid its 1,700 acres of protected land. The Metra railway system serves the western suburbs via the Metra Union Pacific West Line and Burlington Northern Santa Fe Line.

Naperville

Naperville, the oldest town in DuPage County, was settled by Captain Joseph Naper. Soon after, in the late 1830s, settlers of German ancestry came from Pennsylvania to transform the prairie into farmland. Although today's city is at the center of a "research and high technology corridor" and has been cited as one of the fastest-growing suburbs in the nation, Naperville retains something of the atmosphere of a small town with its core of large Victorian houses and beautiful historic district. The downtown shopping area features more than 100 shops and restaurants in historic buildings; it adjoins the Riverwalk, a 3 1/2-mile winding brick pathway along the DuPage River.

Restaurants in Naperville

★ ★ MESON SABIKA (MAP K)

1025 Aurora Ave (60540)
Phone 630/983-3000
Fax 630/983-0715
www.mesonsabika.com
There's no chance of boredom at this colorful Spanish tapas restaurant with eight different ornately decorated dining rooms, an extensive menu of small, shareable dishes, and plenty of sangria. The beautiful 1847 Victorian mansion is surrounded by gardens and has a pleasant outdoor terrace. Spanish, tapas menu. Lunch, dinner, Sun brunch. Closed holidays. Bar. Children's menu. Casual attire. Outdoor seating. **$$**

★ ★ RAFFI'S ON 5TH (MAP K)

200 E 5th Ave (60563)
Phone 630/961-8203
Exposed-brick walls and soaring ceilings create an urban loft setting, fitting for the cosmopolitan Raffi's. Middle Eastern rugs and artwork should tip you off that Raffi's best dishes, despite a pan-Mediterranean menu, hail from that region. Raves go the grilled lamb chops, chicken kebobs, couscous, tabbouleh, and stuffed grape leaves. The sophisticated setting makes this a favored choice for daters. Mediterranean menu. Lunch, dinner. Bar. Casual attire. **$$**

★ ★ SAMBA ROOM (MAP K)

22 E Chicago Ave (60540)
Phone 630/753-0985
Fax 630/753-0992

Loud, brash, and spicy, Samba Room conjures the sexy, free-spirited aura of pre-Castro Cuba. Bossa nova in the air and the potent mojitos freely flowing from the bar make party-hardy patrons feel at home. But foodies will be satisfied too with the cumin-rubbed pork tenderloin, whole fried snapper, and rum-glazed mahi mahi. The serpentine bar and colorful interiors distract diners waiting for tables on weekends. You'll find several sibling Samba Rooms, a small Dallas-based chain, around the country. Latin American menu. Lunch, dinner. Closed Dec 25. Bar. Casual attire. Outdoor seating. **$$**

Oak Brook

Known as Fullersburg in the mid-1800s, Oak Brook is the home of
Butler National Golf Club. Sports and recreation have long been
important in this carefully planned village; it has established and
maintains 12 miles of biking and hiking paths and more than 450
acres of parks and recreation land. Today, Oak Brook is identified as
both a mecca for international polo players and the headquarters of
many major corporations.

Restaurants in Oak Brook

★★ BRAXTON SEAFOOD GRILL (MAP K)

3 Oak Brook Center Mall (60523)
Phone 630/574-2155
Fax 630/574-2256
www.braxtonseafood.com

A mini-chain with several locations nationwide, Braxton Seafood
Grill makes regionally sourced fresh seafood its theme. Lodged in the
Oakbrook Center Mall, Braxton serves shoppers and area office workers a vast menu sure to please most fish lovers. Look for signature
dishes including almond-crusted tilapia, Maryland crabcakes, grilled
swordfish, cioppino seafood stew, and shrimp scampi, as well as live
Maine lobster. Line cooks plating dishes behind the glass-enclosed
kitchen provide entertainment. Seafood menu. Lunch, dinner. Closed
holidays. Bar. Children's menu. **$$$**

★★ FOND DE LA TOUR (MAP K)

40 N Tower Rd (60521)
Phone 630/620-1500
Fax 630/620-1858

Oak Brook's tony French restaurant Fond de la Tour serves up
classic fare in a formal setting to largely special-occasion celebrants.
Nothing on the menu breaks new ground, but the cooking is prac-
ticed, from the overture sweetbreads and oysters Rockefeller to the
encore cherries jubilee. Accomplished tableside service by tuxedoed
waiters warrants ordering Caesar salad, steak tartare, and Dover sole.
French menu. Lunch, dinner. Closed Sun-Mon; holidays. Bar. Casual
attire. Valet parking. **$$$**

Oak Park

Oak Park, one of Chicago's oldest suburbs, is a village of well-kept houses and magnificent trees. The town is internationally famous as the birthplace of Ernest Hemingway and for its concentration of Prairie School houses by Frank Lloyd Wright and other modern architects of the early 20th century. Wright both lived in the town and practiced architecture from his Oak Park studio between 1889 and 1909.

Restaurant in Oak Park

★ ★ CAFÉ LE COQ (MAP K)
734 Lake St (60301)
Phone 708/848-2233

Affordable bistro classics endear Oak Parkers to Café Le Coq. Chef Steven Chiapetti worked at Rhapsody in downtown Chicago before resurfacing with this suburbanite. His lusty cooking distinguishes bistro standards like Lyonnais salad, onion soup, mussels in white wine, and steak frites. Daily changing specials, known as "plat du jour," may include coq au vin. The pleasant storefront is trimmed in French fleur de lis symbols and images of the restaurant's namesake rooster. The wine list, like the food, is reasonably priced. French bistro menu. Dinner. Closed Mon. Bar. Casual attire. Outdoor seating. **$$**

South Suburbs and Northwest Indiana

The suburbs south of Chicago and in northwest Indiana have experienced considerable growth in recent years. Families, in particular, have been drawn to the region, which offers close-knit communities, affordable housing, and beautiful public parks. The region is a short drive from Chicago via Interstate 57 or 94, as well as the Chicago Skyway (I-90). Public transportation to and from Chicago is convenient, with the south suburbs served by the Metra Electric Line and Rock Island District Line, while the South Shore Line runs all the way to South Bend, Indiana, stopping in Hammond, Gary, and Dune Park, among other locations. In the town of Porter, Indiana Dunes National Lakeshore greets nearly 2 million visitors a year to its 15,000 acres of beaches, dunes, wetlands, and forests.

South Suburbs

★ ★ OLD BARN   (MAP J)

8100 S Central Ave, Burbank (60459)
Phone 708/422-5400
www.theoldbarn.biz

First opened in 1921, the Old Barn has been the watering hole for everyone from Charles Lindbergh, Jr., to W. C. Fields. But the fact that they—and a host of other well-known personalities—were once regulars here is not what draws customers. Mouth-watering American classics like filet mignon, T-bone steak, and prime rib so good it has been voted "#1 prime rib" by a local newspaper, are what keep them coming back. Steak menu. Lunch, dinner. Closed holidays. Bar. Children's menu. Valet parking. Casual attire. **$$**

★ PALERMO'S   (MAP J)

4849 W 95th St, Oak Lawn (60453)
Phone 708/425-6262
www.palermos95th.com

This family-run restaurant just southwest of Chicago has been a local favorite for over 30 years. The dimly lit dining room is reminiscent of old-world Italy, and is the perfect atmosphere for either a romantic dinner or a casual night out with the family. The menu of Italian-American fare is sizable and features standards like chicken Vesuvio and veal Parmigiana as well as a variety of pastas and seasonal specials. And if it's pizza you're craving, look no further. Palermo's pizza—regular or thin crust, traditional or Chicago-style deep dish—is renowned throughout the area, and is available for carry-out along with a selection of items from the dining room menu. Italian menu. Lunch, dinner. Closed Tues. Bar. Children's menu. Casual attire. **$$**

★ WHITE FENCE FARM   (MAP K)

11700 Joliet Rd, Lemont (60439)
Phone 630/739-1720
www.whitefencefarm.com

This charming country farmhouse proclaims that it serves "the World's Greatest Chicken." Whether that statement is true or not is up to you, but White Fence Farm has won praises for its fried chicken, which is coated with a secret breading recipe, baked, and then flash fried. Aged steaks and a few fish selections round out the menu of home-style favorites, which are served in ten quaint dining rooms. But more than just a restaurant famous for fried chicken, White Fence Farm is a place to spend the day with the family. On its sprawling grounds are an antique car museum, kiddie rides, and a petting zoo with llamas, sheep, and goats. American menu. Lunch, dinner. Closed Mon; Thanksgiving, Dec 24-25; also Jan. Children's menu. Casual attire. **$$**

★ ★ WHITNEY'S GRILLE 233 (MAP J)
9333 S Cicero Ave, Oak Lawn (60453)
Phone 708/229-8888
www.oaklawn.hilton.com
This casual-elegant restaurant in the Hilton Oak Lawn feels more like a beloved neighborhood place than a hotel restaurant. American menu. Breakfast, lunch, dinner. Bar. Children's menu. **$$**

Northwest Indiana

★ BILLY JACK'S CAFÉ AND GRILL (MAP K)

2904 N Calumet Ave, Valparaiso (46383)
Phone 219/477-3797

Billy Jack's is an amalgam of all that's spicy from Italy and Mexico. With ingredients scoured daily from local markets, this innovative restaurant is a must-see in Valparaiso. Italian, Southwestern menu. Lunch, dinner. Bar. Children's menu. Casual attire. **$$**

★ BISTRO 157 (MAP K)

157 Lincolnway, Valparaiso (46383)
Phone 219/462-0992

Bistro 157 burst onto the scene only a few years ago but brought with it the notion of an American bistro. Utilizing ingredients from all over the globe, Bistro 157 delights customers with everything from sushi to short ribs. Eclectic/International menu. Lunch, dinner. Closed Mon. Casual attire. Outdoor seating. **$$**

★ ★ CAFÉ ELISE (MAP J)

435 Ridge Rd, Munster (46321)
Phone 219/836-2233

A relative newcomer to the northwest Indiana dining scene, Café Elise has drawn crowds for its innovative modern American cuisine. American menu. Closed Mon. Lunch, dinner. Bar. Children's menu. Casual attire. **$$**

★ ★ CAFÉ VENEZIA (MAP K)

405 W 81st Ave, Merrillville (46410)
Phone 219/736-2203

For more than a decade, Café Venezia has set the standard for authentic regional Italian cuisine. The extensive wine list and unfussy presentations delight guests night after night. Italian menu. Closed Sun. Lunch, dinner. Casual attire. **$$**

★ ★ ★ CLAYTON'S 238 (MAP K)

66 W Lincolnway, Valparaiso (46383)
Phone 219/531-0612

Behind this vintage storefront lies one of the pioneers of northwest Indiana's fine dining scene. Self-taught chef William Potts opened Clayton's in the mid-1990s, when words like truffles and foie gras made diners a bit apprehensive. But almost a decade later, things have changed in Valparaiso. The refined New American menu, which has included such dishes as foie gras dumplings and wild rice risotto, keeps customers coming back and continues to set the standard for northwest Indiana dining. American menu. Dinner. Closed Sun-Mon. Casual attire. Outdoor seating. **$$**

★ ★ DISH RESTAURANT (MAP K)
3907 Calumet Ave, Valparaiso (46383)
Phone 219/465-9221
More than just your average local eatery, Dish takes American comfort food to a new level. Utilizing seasonal, locally grown ingredients, chef/owner Erick Staresina gives old favorites like meat loaf and ribs an upscale twist. The concept has quickly become a favorite of locals, who enjoy the extensive wine list as well as the bright, modern, and unpretentious atmosphere. American menu. Lunch, dinner. Closed Sun. Bar. Casual attire. **$$**

★ DON QUIXOTE (MAP K)
119 E Lincolnway, Valparaiso (46383)
Phone 219/462-7976
For the only authentic Spanish cuisine in northwest Indiana, you must go to Don Quixote. The paella is still amazing after more than 15 years of continuous trailblazing. Spanish menu. Lunch, dinner. Closed Sun. Children's menu. Casual attire. Reservations recommended. Outdoor seating. **$$**

★ ★ LUCREZIA (MAP K)
428 S Calumet Rd, Chesterton (46304)
Phone 219/926-5829
www.lucreziacafe.com
Lucrezia is a tiny gem of a find where the locals go for excellent northern Italian cuisine. Don't forget to try the incredible bruschetta! Italian menu. Lunch, dinner. Bar. Casual attire. Outdoor seating. **$$**

★ ★ ★ MILLER BAKERY CAFÉ (MAP K)
555 S Lake St, Gary (46403)
Phone 219/938-2229
Located in the Miller Beach area, this charming restaurant's name comes from its setting in a renovated bakery building. The kitchen serves up mostly modern American fare, with specialties including pasta and seafood dishes. American menu. Lunch, dinner. Closed Mon. Casual attire. Reservations recommended on weekends. **$$**

★ ★ PHIL SMIDT'S ⬤243 (MAP J)

1205 N Calumet Ave, Hammond (46320)
Phone 219/659-0025; toll-free 800/376-4534
Fax 219/659-6955
www.froglegs.com
This landmark restaurant continues to be popular after more than
90 years of continuous operation. What would be considered retro
at other restaurants is just the way it's always been at Phil's, where
steaks and seafood are upstaged by the incredible frog's legs. Seafood
menu. Lunch, dinner. Closed Mon; holidays. Bar. Children's menu.
Casual attire. **$$**

★ ★ STRONGBOW INN ⬤244 (MAP K)

2405 E Rte 30, Valparaiso (46383)
Phone 219/531-0162
For more than 50 years, the Strongbow Inn has been delighting diners
from all over the country. While known primarily for the amazing
turkey specialties, the expanded menu has much more to offer.
American menu. Lunch, dinner. Bar. Children's menu. Casual attire.
$$

Groceries and Markets

CHICAGO

Aion
2135 W Division St
Phone 773/489-1534
Market selling high-end bulk teas.

Alliance Bakery
1736 W Division St
Phone 773/278-0366
www.alliance-bakery.com
Good Eastern European bakery.

Arirang Supermarket
4017 W Lawrence Ave
Phone 312/777-2400
Korean market in the Uptown neighborhood.

Armitage Produce
3334 W Armitage Ave
Phone 773/486-8133
Mexican grocery with a good produce selection.

Art Gallery Kafe
1907 N Milwaukee Ave
Phone 773/235-2351
Great café specializing in sweets and pastries.

Artopolis Bakery, Café, and Agora
306 S Halsted St
Phone 312/559-9000
www.artopolischicago.com
Excellent Greektown bakery.

Athens Grocery
324 S Halsted St
Phone 312/454-0940
Greektown imported specialty foods.

Brasil Legal
2153 N Western Ave
Imported Brazilian foods, appetizers, and feijoada on request.

California Milwaukee Produce
2294 N Milwaukee Ave
Phone 773/486-5905
Mexican grocery that sells produce.

Carniceria Roman
2633 W Armitage Ave
Phone 773/772-4049
Great selection of South American produce and an extremely loyal local clientele.

Cermak Produce
2701 W North Ave
Phone 773/278-4447
Big Mexican grocery store with a great produce department.

Chicago Food Corp/Joong Boo Market
3333 N Kimball Ave
Phone 773/478-5566
www.chicagofood.com
Great Asian/Korean grocery store.

Chicago Food Market
2245 S Wentworth Ave
Phone 312/842-4361
Traditional Chinese grocery.

Coffee and Tea Exchange
3311 N Broadway St
Phone 773/528-2241
www.coffeeandtea.com
Good wholesale coffee and tea.

Cooking Fools
1916 W North Ave
Phone 773/276-5565
Gourmet deli with great chocolate and amazing homemade mango habañero sorbet.

Daley Plaza Farmers' Market
Washington and Dearborn sts
Phone 312/744-9187
June-Oct: Thurs
Features organic and sustainable agriculture.

Devon Market
1440 W Devon Ave
Phone 773/338-2572
Good produce and inexpensive ethnic foods.

Dirk's Fish and Gourmet Shop
2070 N Clybourn Ave
Phone 773/404-3475
www.dirksfish.com
Best fishmonger in all of Chicago.

Dubby's
2108 W Division St
Phone 773/645-7100
Upscale bulk and specialty foods.

Family Fruit Market
4118 N Cicero Ave
Phone 773/481-2500
Good selection of produce and a great deli.

Fox & Obel
401 E Illinois St
Phone 312/410-7301
www.fox-obel.com
Upscale deli with gourmet foodstuffs.

Green City Market
Lincoln Park along LaSalle St
www.chicagogreencitymarket.org
May-Oct: Wed
Known as "Chicago's only sustainable green market."

Hyde Park Co-op
1526 E 55th St
Phone 773/667-1444
Expensive vegan deli.

Intelligentsia
3123 N Broadway St
Phone 773/348-8058
www.intelligentsiacoffee.com
Many restaurants and cafés serve coffees from this great local roaster.

J's Vitamins and More
5316 N Milwaukee Ave
Phone 773/763-1917
Health food store with great prices.

Jimenez
2140 N Western Ave
Phone 773/235-0999
One of several Mexican groceries throughout the city with good prices.

Kolatek's
2445 N Harlem Ave
Phone 773/637-3772
Polish bakery and deli.

Leonidas
231 S LaSalle St
Phone toll-free 888/536-6432
www.worldofchocolate.com
Belgian chocolatier with decadent treats.

Letizia's Natural Bakery
2146 W Division St
Phone 773/342-1011
www.superyummy.com
Bakery and café that emphasizes
sustainable agriculture.

Los Artista
California and Armitage aves
Late hours and a great selection.

Los Cuatro Caminos
2722 N Milwaukee Ave
Phone 773/384-0116
Mexican grocery with great
produce.

Margie's Candies
1960 N Western Ave
Phone 773/384-1035
www.margiescandies.
Old-fashioned ice cream
shop and candy store where
everything is homemade.

Maxwell Street Market
Canal St and Roosevelt Rd
Phone 312/922-3100
Sun
A Chicago tradition with a wide
variety of ethnic produce and
foodstuffs.

Moonstruck
320 N Michigan Ave
Phone 312/696-1201
www.moonstruckchocolate.com
Indulge in handcrafted artisan
chocolates and a Moon shake.

Niko's Produce
2101 N Milwaukee Ave
Phone 773/252-4920
Inexpensive Mexican grocery.

Nuts on Clark
3830 N Clark St
Phone 773/549-6622
www.nutsonclark.com
Popular spot for fresh nuts, dried
fruits, gourmet popcorn, and
candies.

Panaderia La Central
2218 N California Ave
Traditional Mexican baked goods.

Perk-U-Later
2466 W Armitage Ave
Phone 773/252-0082
Local café with good coffee.

Pete's Food Mart
2556 W Armitage Ave
Phone 773/772-5148
Independent grocery store.

Red Hen Bakery
1623 N Milwaukee Ave
Phone 773/342-6823
Amazing gourmet breads and
baked goods used in many local
restaurants.

Sherwyn's
645 W Diversey Pkwy
Phone 773/477-1934
Large health and natural foods
store.

Stanley's Fruits & Vegetables
1558 N Elston Ave
Phone 773/276-8050
Good selection of inexpensive
quality produce.

Sultan's Market
2057 W North Ave
Phone 773/235-3072
Middle Eastern deli that draws
many vegetarians.

Sweet Thang
1921 W North Ave
Phone 773/772-4166
www.sweetthangcakes.com
Traditional French patisserie.

**Ten Ren Tea and Ginseng
Company**
2247 S Wentworth Ave
Phone 312/842-1171
One-of-a-kind Chinatown
tea shop with more than 100
varieties of tea.

Treasure Island
2121 N Clybourn Ave
Phone 773/880-8880
Family-owned grocery that offers
many hard-to-find European
items.

Vosges Haut-Chocolat
520 N Michigan Ave
Phone 312/644-9450
Also at The Peninsula Chicago
108 E Superior St
Phone 312/335-9858
www.vosgeschocolate.com
Haute chocolate shop with
exotic flavor pairings.

Wong's Food City
222 W 26th St
Phone 312/808-9635
South Chinatown grocery with
good prices.

SUBURBS

Angelo Caputo's
510 W Lake St, Addison
Phone 630/543-0151
www.caputomarkets.com
Inexpensive Italian grocery with
a huge produce selection and a
great butcher counter.

Casey's Market
*915 Burlington Ave,
Western Springs*
Phone 708/246-0380
Great prepared foods.

Casteel Coffee
2924 Central Ave, Evanston
Phone 847/424-9999; toll-free
877/560-8335
www.casteelcoffee.com
Small-batch specialty coffee
roasters.

Diho Market
*6120 W Dempster St, Morton
Grove*
Phone 847/965-8688
Authentic Japanese food market.

E & M Meat Market
3358 Dempster St, Skokie
Phone 847/679-6950
Excellent butcher shop.

Judy's Bakery
706 Main St, Evanston
Phone 847/475-6565
A local treat.

Mitsuwa
100 E Algonquin Rd, Arlington Heights
Phone 847/956-6699
Huge Japanese market with an unbelievable fish selection.

Piron
500 Main St, Evanston
Phone 847/864-5504
Excellent handmade Belgian chocolates.

Pita Inn Market
3910 Dempster St, Skokie
Phone 847/677-0211
www.pitainn.com
Freshly made hummus and baba ghanoush.

The Spice House
1941 Central St, Evanston
Phone 847/328-3711
www.thespicehouse.com
Sells spices and herbs as well as mills and spice accessories.

50 Spots to Have a Drink

Alumni Club
15 W Division St
Phone 312/337-4349
www.alumniclubchicago.com
Twentysomethings flock to this college sports-themed bar to dance the night away or watch their favorite sporting event.

Andy's Jazz Club
11 E Hubbard St
Phone 312/642-6805
www.andysjazzclub.com
A casual, friendly place to hear live jazz.

The Bar at Peninsula Chicago Hotel
108 E Superior St
Phone 312/337-2888
chicago.peninsula.com
A stylish, sophisticated crowd is drawn to this updated martini bar.

Bar Louie
226 W Chicago Ave
Phone 312/337-3313
www.barlouieamerica.com
Delicious pub grub and a funky atmosphere.

Big Bar
151 E Wacker Dr
Phone 312/565-1234
chicagoregency.hyatt.com
This bar in the Hyatt Regency Chicago lives up to its name, with a 160-foot bar and drinks almost as large.

Blyss
1061 W Madison St
Phone 312/433-0013
Everyone from hipsters to young professionals to sports fans comes to this west-side spot for the ritzy yet unpretentious atmosphere.

Burton Place
1447 N Wells St
Phone 312/664-4699
This neighborhood sports bar/lounge has been a favorite of comedians from nearby Second City since the early 1980s.

Butch McGuire's
20 W Division St
Phone 312/787-3984
This Irish pub is one of the oldest of the Division Street bars, but is still a singles mecca.

Café Allure
1501 N Dayton St
Phone 312/55-8731
Fashion-conscious waitstaff and DJs spinning a mix of house and jazz raise the cool quotient at this mellow hangout.

Celtic Crossings
751 N Clark St
Phone 312/337-1005
The owners of this pub hail from the Emerald Isle, making it an authentic Irish bar.

Clark Street Ale House
742 N Clark St
Phone 312/642-9253
Beer lovers can choose
from over 90 handcrafted
microbrews at this spacious
River North pub.

Coq d'Or
140 E Walton Pl
Phone 312/787-2200
dining.thedrakehotel.com
A sophisticated lounge in
the Drake Hotel with a
relaxed atmosphere and
perfect martinis.

Corosh
1072 N Milwaukee Ave
Phone 773/235-0600
www.corosh.com
Come to this casual
neighborhood bar/restaurant
for a cocktail or two or for a
dinner of Italian favorites.

**Encore Lunch Club and
Liquid Lounge**
171 W Randolph St
Phone 312/338-3788
Dark amber lighting, velvet
drapes, and Art Deco touches
set the scene for this chic lounge
in the Hotel Allegro.

Fadó Irish Pub
100 W Grand Ave
Phone 312/836-0066
www.fadoirishpub.com
The bartenders here take
their time pouring a pint of
Guinness—the true sign of an
authentic Irish pub.

Finn McCool's
15 W Division St
Phone 312/37-4349
This Irish-themed bar offers a
more laid-back setting than its
upstairs neighbor, Alumni Club.

Fulton Lounge
955 W Fulton Market
Phone 312/942-9500
www.fultonlounge.com
Local residents of the Fulton
Street Market area and diners
from nearby Randolph Street
restaurants head here for
cocktails and a low-key setting.

Ghost Bar
440 W Randolph St
Phone 312/575-9900
www.n9ne.com
Overlooking the dining room of
Nine restaurant, this sleek lounge
is a retreat for the young and
beautiful.

Govnor's Pub
207 N State St
Phone 312/236-3693
www.govnors.com
The after-work crowd comes to
this Loop pub to enjoy a menu
of traditional Irish and American
favorites paired with pints of
Guinness.

Grape Street and Vine
226 E Ontario St
Phone 312/642-7440
Those who want to avoid the
rowdy twentysomething crowd
come to this piano bar to relax
and enjoy the jazzy atmosphere.

Harry's Velvet Room
56 W Illinois St
Phone 312/527-5600
If you want to get rid of some extra cash, this swanky wine and champagne bar is the place to go.

Ice Bar
738 N Clark St
Phone 312/440-8841
Funky décor and an enticing variety of martinis make this one of the trendier River North spots.

Iggy's
700 N Milwaukee Ave
Phone 312/829-4449
With a restaurant on the main level and a lounge upstairs, this low-lit nightspot offers a wide selection of deluxe martinis as well as late-night munchies.

Jaks Tap
901 W Jackson Blvd
Phone 312/666-1700
www.jakstap.com
With 40 beers on tap and seemingly almost as many televisions, this bar is a popular hangout for sports fans.

Joe's
940 W Weed St
Phone 312/337-3486
www.joesbar.com
A lively sports bar with a 200-seat outdoor beer garden.

Kasey's Tavern
701 S Dearborn
Phone 312/427-7992
www.kaseystavern.com
Friendly bartenders and a warm atmosphere make this 115-year-old tavern a favorite with Printer's Row residents.

Kaz Bar
333 Dearborn St
Phone 312/45-0333
www.kazbarchicago.com
Settle into one of the plush couches with Moroccan-inspired canopies at this colorful lounge in the House of Blues Hotel.

Kitty O'Shea's
720 S Michigan Ave
Phone 312/922-4400
www.chicagohilton.com
A bit of the Emerald Isle in the South Loop's Hilton hotel.

Le Bar
20 E Chestnut St
Phone 312/324-4000
www.sofitel.com
This sleek lounge in the Sofitel attracts a mature, sophisticated crowd.

Le Passage
937 N Rush St
Phone 312/255-0022
When you see the rich and beautiful lined up behind velvet ropes in an alleyway, you know you've found the entrance to this clubby Gold Coast hideaway.

Le Rendez-Vous
520 N Michigan Ave
Phone 312/645-1500
www.lemeridien.com
Le Meridien hotel's colorful and
elegant Parisian-style bar.

The Lodge Tavern
21 W Division St
Phone 312/642-4406
This mainstay of the Division
Street singles scene has been
known to attract local sports
figures.

Martini Ranch
311 W Chicago Ave
Phone 312/335-9500
This bar serves up strong
varieties of the drink for which
it's named.

The Matchbox
770 N Milwaukee Ave
Phone 312/666-9292
Appropriately named—its 20
barstools almost touch the
back wall, forcing patrons
to abandon any hopes for
personal space.

Melvin B's
1114 N State St
Phone 312/751-9897
The city's most popular outdoor
patio bar.

Minx
111 W Hubbard St
Phone 312/828-9000
DJs spin French disco and down-
tempo house at this stylish
restaurant/lounge/club.

Monk's Pub
205 W Lake St
Phone 312/357-6665
A popular burgers 'n' beer spot
with Loop workers.

Narcisse
710 N Clark St
877/834-2617
www.narcisse.us
This hip hotspot offers decadent
champagne cocktails and swanky
décor.

O'Callaghan's
29 W Hubbard St
Phone 312/527-1180
www.ocallaghanspub.com
This friendly Irish pub features
plenty of TVs for watching the
big game.

Old Town Ale House
219 W North Ave
Phone 312/944-7020
Located across the street from
Piper's Alley movie theater and
Second City, this cozy pub is a
popular choice for post-show
drinks.

Old Town Pub
1339 N Wells St
Phone 312/266-6789
The no-frills atmosphere—
pizza, beer, and the game on
TV—attracts everyone from the
sporty to the hip.

Pepper Canister
509 N Wells St
Phone 312/467-3300
This upscale Irish pub offers ice-cold drafts and contemporary versions of favorites like shepherd's pie and fish-and-chips.

Pippin's Tavern
806 N Rush St
Phone 312/787-5435
This small, rustic bar boasts the oldest liquor license on Rush Street.

Signature Lounge
875 N Michigan Ave
Phone 312/787 7230
www.signatureroom.com
Enjoy the best view of the city at this lounge on the 96th floor of the Hancock building.

Sonotheque
1444 W Chicago Ave
Phone 312/226-7600
www.sonotheque.org
This modern lounge features local and international DJs spinning everything from techno to hip-hop.

Sugar
108 W Kinzie St
Phone 312/822-9999
A swanky "dessert bar" that also functions as a nightclub.

Tantrum
1023 S State St
Phone 312/939-9160
This romantic martini bar in the South Loop attracts a hip, professional crowd.

The Tasting Room at Randolph Wine Cellars
1415 W Randolph St
Phone 312/942-1212
tlcwine.com
Choose from over 100 wines to order by the glass, bottle, or flight.

Whiskey Bar & Grill
1015 N Rush St
Phone 312/475 0300
Stand elbow-to-elbow with a see-and-be-seen crowd.

Whiskey Blue
172 W Adams St
Phone 312/782-4933
The W Chicago City Center's luxe lounge attracts a sophisticated after-work crowd.

Budget-Friendly Restaurants

CHICAGO

A La Turka, 20

Abu Nawas, 20

Ann Sather, 21

Arco de Cuchilleros, 22

Calliope Café, 28

Chicago Diner, 33

Ed Debevic's, 35

Hema's Kitchen, 42

Oak Tree, 53

Orange, 54

Parthenon, 80

Penny's Noodle Shop, 56

Piece, 81

Pizzeria Uno, 56

Pot Pan, 81

Toast, 84

SUBURBS

Carmen's, *Evanston*, 88

Michael's Restaurant, *Highland Park*, 94

Walker Brothers Original Pancake House, *Wilmette*, 100

Romantic Restaurants

CHICAGO

SUBURBS

Family-Friendly Restaurants

CHICAGO

Adobo Grill, 20	Mon Ami Gabi, 50
Atwood Café, 12	Naniwa, 52
Avenues, 22	Nick's Fishmarket, 15
Bandera, 22	Nix, 52
The Berghoff, 13	Oak Tree, 53
Bluepoint Oyster Bar, 73	Orange, 54
Caliterra, 28	Papagus Greek Taverna, 55
Calliope Café, 28	Parthenon, 80
Cerise, 31	Pizzeria Uno, 56
Club Lucky, 75	Ras Dashen, 57
Ed Debevic's, 35	Redfish, 58
Eli's the Place for Steak, 37	Riva, 58
Glory, 76	Roy's, 58
Harry Caray's, 41	Santorini, 82
Joe's Be-Bop Café, 43	She She, 62
John's Place, 43	Tizi Melloul, 64
Maggiano's, 47	Toast, 84
Mia Francesca, 49	Tucci Benucch, 66
Mike Ditka's, 50	Wishbone, 86

SUBURBS

94th Aero Squadron, *Wheeling*, 110

Bob Chinn's Crab House, *Wheeling*, 110

Braxton Seafood Grill, *Oak Brook*, 115

Café Central, *Highland Park*, 93

Country Inn Restaurant at Lambs Farm, *Libertyville*, 105

Don Quixote, *Valparaiso, IN*, 121

Don's Fishmarket, *Skokie*, 89

The English Room, *Lake Forest*, 97

Merle's #1 Barbecue, *Evanston*, 90

Meson Sabika, *Naperville*, 113

Michael's Restaurant, *Highland Park*, 94

MK North, *Glenview*, 104

Nick's Fishmarket, *Rosemont*, 109

Palermo's, *Oak Lawn*, 118

Palm Court, *Arlington Heights*, 102

Phil Smidt's, *Munster, IN*, 122

Prairie Moon, *Evanston*, 91

Retro Bistro, *Arlington Heights*, 103

Strongbow Inn, *Valparaiso, IN*, 122

Tonelli's, *Northbrook*, 107

Walker Brothers Original Pancake House, *Wilmette*, 100

Whitney's Grille, *Oak Lawn*, 119

Restaurants That Are Good for Groups

CHICAGO

A La Turka, 20

Adobo Grill, 20

Ann Sather, 21

Arco de Cuchilleros, 22

Aria, 12

Azure, 72

Bandera, 22

Basta Pasta, 24

Bin 36, 25

Brasserie Jo, 25

Brett's, 26

Bricks, 26

Butterfield 8, 26

Café Ba-Ba-Reeba!, 27

Café Iberico, 27

The Capital Grille, 31

Carmine's, 31

Cerise, 31

Chicago Chop House, 32

Chilpancingo, 33

Club Lucky, 75

Cyrano's Bistrot and Wine Bar, 34

Ed Debevic's, 35

Erwin, 38

Fogo de Chão, 39

Frontera Grill, 39

Gene & Georgetti, 40

Gioco, 14

Harry Caray's, 41

Heaven on Seven on Rush, 42

Indian Garden, 42

Joe's Be-Bop Café, 43

La Bocca della Verita, 45

La Strada, 14

SUBURBS

94th Aero Squadron, *Wheeling*, 110

Carlucci, *Rosemont*, 108

Carmen's, *Evanston*, 88

The Dining Room at Kendall College, *Evanston*, 88

Las Palmas, *Evanston*, 88

Merle's #1 Barbecue, *Evanston*, 90

Oceanique, *Evanston*, 91

Palm Court, *Arlington Heights*, 102

Palermo's, *Oak Lawn*, 118

Periyali Greek Taverna, *Glenview*, 104

Pete Miller's Steakhouse, *Evanston*, 91

Phil Smidt's, *Munster, IN*, 122

Prairie Moon, *Evanston*, 91

Strongbow Inn, *Valparaiso, IN*, 122

White Fence Farm, *Lemont*, 118

Va Pensiero, *Evanston*, 92

Quiet Restaurants

CHICAGO

Ambria, 21

Arun's, 71

Avenues, 22

Café Bernard, 27

Cantare, 28

Cerise, 31

Chez Joel, 74

Chilpancingo, 33

Crofton on Wells, 34

The Dining Room, 35

Dinotto Ristorante, 35

Erawan, 38

Ixcapuzalco, 76

Jane's, 76

La Creperie, 45

La Sardine, 77

La Tache, 45

Les Nomades, 46

NoMi, 53

Pili Pili, 56

Seasons, 60

Spiaggia, 62

Spring, 84

SUBURBS

Betise, *Wilmette*, 99

Café La Café, *Des Plaines*, 108

Café Le Coq, *Oak Park*, 116

Campagnola, *Evanston*, 88

Carlos', *Highland Park*, 93

Clayton's, *Valparaiso, IN*, 120

Fond de la Tour, *Oak Brook*, 115

Gabriel's, *Highwood*, 96

Le Titi de Paris, *Arlington Heights*, 102

Oceanique, *Evanston*, 91

Trio, *Evanston*, 92

Va Pensiero, *Evanston*, 92

Restaurants That Serve Brunch

CHICAGO

Adobo Grill, 20

Ann Sather, 21

Arco de Cuchilleros, 22

Atwood Café, 12

Avenues, 22

Bongo Room, 73

Brett's, 26

Carmine's, 31

Cerise, 31

Coobah, 34

The Dining Room, 35

Erwin, 38

Flo, 75

Frontera Grill, 39

Ixcapuzalco, 76

Jane's, 76

Joe's Be-Bop Café, 43

John's Place, 43

Meritage, 78

Mike Ditka's, 50

MOD, 79

Nix, 52

North Pond, 53

Orange, 54

Pump Room, 57

Salpicon, 59

Seasons, 60

Signature Room at the 95th, 62

Szechwan East, 64

Toast, 84

Wishbone, 86

SUBURBS

94th Aero Squadron, *Wheeling,* 110

Betise, *Wilmette,* 99

Billy Jack's, *Valparaiso, IN,* 120

Country Inn Restaurant at Lambs Farm, *Libertyville,* 105

The English Room, *Lake Forest,* 97

Jilly's Café, *Evanston,* 89

Meson Sabika, *Naperville,* 113

Prairie Moon, *Evanston,* 91

Strongbow Inn, *Valparaiso, IN,* 122

Whitney's Grille, *Oak Lawn,* 119

Restaurants with Outdoor Seating

CHICAGO

A La Turka, 20

Adobo Grill, 20

Arco de Cuchilleros, 22

Atlantique, 22

Atwood Café, 12

Avec, 72

Azuré, 72

Basta Pasta, 24

Bice, 25

Blackbird, 72

Blue Fin, 73

Bluepoint Oyster Bar, 73

Bob San, 73

Brasserie Jo, 25

Brett's, 26

Butterfield 8, 26

Café Ba-Ba-Reeba!, 27

Café Bernard, 27

Café Iberico, 27

Calliope Café, 28

Cerise, 31

Chez Joel, 74

Chicago Chop House, 32

Coco Pazzo, 33

Como, 75

Coobah, 34

Cyrano's Bistro and Wine Bar, 34

Dinotto Ristorante, 35

Frontera Grill, 39

Glory, 76

Hatsuhana, 41

Jane's, 76

Japonais, 42

Joe's Be-Bop Café, 43

Keefer's, 44

Kevin, 44

SUBURBS

Restaurants for Business Meals

CHICAGO

Aria, 12

Ambria, 21

Avenues, 22

Bin 36, 25

Bob San, 75

Brasserie Jo, 25

Cantare, 28

The Capital Grille, 31

Charlie Trotter's, 32

Coco Pazzo, 33

Crofton on Wells, 34

Everest, 14

Gibson's Steakhouse, 40

Keefer's, 44

Kevin, 44

Marche, 77

Mike Ditka's, 50

mk, 50

Nick's Fishmarket, 15

NoMi, 53

Pane Caldo, 54

Pili Pili, 56

Rushmore, 82

Seasons, 60

Shanghai Terrace, 61

Signature Room at the 95th, 62

Spiaggia, 62

Tru, 65

SUBURBS

Betise, *Wilmette*, 99

Café Central, *Highland Park*, 93

Café le Coq, *Oak Park*, 116

Campagnola, *Evanston*, 88

Clayton's, *Valparaiso, IN*, 120

Dish, *Valparaiso, IN*, 121

Fond de la Tour, *Oak Brook*, 115

Lucky Platter, *Evanston*, 90

Miller Bakery Café, *Gary, IN*, 122

Strongbow Inn, *Valparaiso, IN*, 122

Va Pensiero, *Evanston*, 92

Restaurants with Unique Décor

CHICAGO

Aria, 12

Atlantique, 22

Café Ba-Ba-Reeba!, 27

Chilpancingo, 33

Club Lucky, 75

Coobah, 34

Ed Debevic's, 35

Erawan, 38

Frontera Grill, 39

Harry Caray's, 41

Heaven on Seven on Rush, 42

Japonais, 42

Joe's Be-Bop Cafe, 43

Marche, 77

MOD, 79

Opera, 16

Orange, 54

Red Light, 81

Salpicon, 59

Souk, 83

Sushi Samba Rio, 63

Tizi Melloul, 64

SUBURBS

94th Aero Squadron, *Wheeling*, 110

Bistro 157, *Valparaiso, IN*, 120

Café la Cave, *Rosemont*, 108

Ceiling Zero, *Northbrook*, 106

Clayton's, *Valparaiso, IN*, 120

Don Quixote, *Valparaiso, IN*, 121

Lucky Platter, *Evanston*, 90

Special-Occasion Restaurants

CHICAGO

Ambria, 21

Aria, 12

Arun's, 71

Atlantique, 22

Avenues, 22

Bin 36, 25

Charlie Trotter's, 32

Chilpancingo, 33

Crofton on Wells, 34

The Dining Room, 35

Erewan, 38

Everest, 14

Fogo de Chão, 39

Frontera Grill, 39

Japonais, 42

Keefer's, 44

Kevin, 44

Le Colonial, 46

Les Nomades, 46

Marche, 77

mk, 50

NoMi, 53

one sixtyblue, 80

Opera, 16

Pili Pili, 56

Seasons, 60

Spiaggia, 62

Spring, 84

Sushi Samba Rio, 63

Tizi Melloul, 64

Tru, 65

Vong's Thai Kitchen, 68

Zealous, 69

SUBURBS

Café Central, *Highland Park*, 93

Café le Coq, *Oak Park*, 116

Campagnola, *Evanston*, 88

Carlos', *Highland Park*, 93

Clayton's, *Valparaiso, IN*, 120

Gabriel's, *Highwood*, 96

Le Titi de Paris, *Arlington Heights*, 102

Miller Bakery Café, *Gary, IN*, 121

Oceanique, *Evanston*, 91

Trio, *Evanston*, 92

Hip & Trendy Restaurants

Fun Finds

Index

I **166**   INDEX

Index by Cuisine

Notes

Notes

Notes

Notes

Notes

Notes

Notes